**Interviewing and Communication
in Social Work**

LIBRARY OF SOCIAL WORK

GENERAL EDITOR : NOEL TIMMS

Professor of Applied Social Studies,
University of Bradford

Interviewing and Communication in Social Work

edited by

Crispin P. Cross

Department of Social Sciences,
North East London Polytechnic

Routledge & Kegan Paul
London and Boston

First published in 1974
by Routledge & Kegan Paul Ltd
Broadway House, 68-74 Carter Lane,
London EC4V 5EL and
9 Park Street,
Boston, Mass. 02108, USA
Set in ten point Pilgrim on eleven point body
and printed in Great Britain by
Northumberland Press Limited,
Gateshead
© C. P. Cross 1974
No part of this book may be reproduced in
any form without permission from the
publisher, except for the quotation of brief
passages in criticism

ISBN 0 7100 7879 x (c)
     0 7100 7880 3 (p)

Library of Congress Catalog Card No. 74-77194

General editor's introduction

The Library of Social Work is designed to meet the needs of students following courses of training for social work. In recent years the number and kinds of training have increased in an unprecedented way. The Library will consist of short texts designed to introduce the student to the main features of each topic of enquiry, to the significant theoretical contributions so far made to its understanding, and to some of the outstanding problems. Each volume will suggest ways in which the student might continue his work by further reading.

   This book is based on at least two firm convictions: that the good interviewer can be made better and a poor interviewer improved, and that such change can come about—in significant part—as the result of acquiring knowledge. Knowledge about interviews, interviewers and interviewees spans a wide range and it is the aim of this book, composed as a series of contributions from different authors, to present that knowledge in digestible form. The interview is approached generally in this study and is described 'as a framework of communication which involves two sets of persons in an encounter whose objectives are usually related to the procurement of factual information, diagnosis and therapy'. The book is organized into two main parts, the first dealing in a number of chapters with, broadly speaking, the socio-cultural context and components of the interview; whilst the second looks more at the techniques of interviewing, its non-verbal aspects, practical considerations, and interviewing in special situations. This division of subject matter is, of course, for organizational convenience—the two sets of considerations are simply aspects of the same complex process. The fact that any discussion claiming adequacy, even at the level of introduction, has to span a range of knowledge helps us to understand the complexity of the interview and, for example, the notion Bogardus has that the interview can result in a *spiral* of understanding and rapport.

In social work literature and in training interviewing tends to be approached somewhat indirectly. It seems, sometimes at any rate, as if direct and systematic learning about interviewing is seen as distracting attention away from the relationship and as endorsing or even inculcating a kind of manipulation. It is certainly time that social work education faced interviewing squarely and considered how best it could be taught. At least one good side-effect of this is, as the authors state, that social workers consider a whole set of issues in communication and also such questions as 'What do you mean by techniques?'

Contents

CONTENTS

Figures and tables

Figures

Tables

Acknowledgments

Communication and interviewing are central to the work of the social worker and the psychotherapist, yet little attempt has been made to explore their interrelationship and their complexity. This book is presented in the hope that the clear interplay between the two in social work will be better appreciated. The experienced social worker, by dint of hard labour in the field, may recognize that interviewing must play a crucial role in the practice of his profession; he may, nevertheless, have under-estimated the extent to which psychological and sociological processes are built into its use. This book is aimed at demonstrating to both the social work student in training and to his more experienced colleague that interviewing and communication together provide the general framework within which casework can be undertaken.

The inspiration for this work came from the authors' participation in a series of courses run by the Department of Social Sciences of the North East London Polytechnic in association with a number of social work organizations. The increasing demand for these courses indicates a gap in the literature which this book aims to fill.

The authors would like to express their appreciation to many social workers with whom they have explored various aspects of interviewing and communication. Many of them will recognize that valuable morsels of their thoughts have been incorporated into our discussion. The authors are also grateful to the Probation and After-care Service whose interest in interviewing and communication provided the initial stimulus for this work. In this connection, special mention must be made of Mrs J. Blooman who encouraged the enterprise in many ways from its inception.

The Director of the North East London Polytechnic and the Head of the Department of Social Sciences also encouraged the enterprise by placing the facilities of the college at our disposal. Dr Claire

ACKNOWLEDGMENTS

Bland, Dr Gordon Smith (now of the LSE) and Mrs C. T. Wilson
took valuable time off their numerous duties to read through
sections of the earlier drafts of the manuscript and made helpful
suggestions for its improvement. We are grateful to them for their
generous co-operation. Ellen Gomes skilfully converted reams of
illegible handwriting into polished typescript within a short period
of time. Nevertheless, all responsibility for the ideas expressed in
the following pages must necessarily fall on the authors alone.

xiv

Note on contributors

C. P. CROSS, B.Sc. (soc.), M.Sc. (econ.), Ph.D. received his training at the London School of Economics and the Regent Street Polytechnic, London. He has taught at the Regent Street Polytechnic, the London School of Economics and now teaches at the North East London Polytechnic, where he is also co-ordinator of research within the Department of Social Sciences.

DIANA LAURENSON, B.Sc. (soc.), Ph.D. also trained at the Regent Street Polytechnic and at the London School of Economics, University of London. She teaches at the North East London Polytechnic where she is also Senior Lecturer in Social Science.

BRIAN W. STRUTT is a Clinical Psychologist. He was trained in Canada and holds the B.A. degree from Waterloo Lutheran University and the M.A. from McMaster University in Canada. He practised psychotherapy in Canada and has taught at the North East London Polytechnic. He now practises in London. He is a member of the British Psychological Society.

MISS SHEILA RAVEN is a trained PSW and is attached, as a social worker, to Holloway Prison in London.

I

Interviewing and communication

Interviewing constitutes an important part of the package of techniques which the social worker, the sociologist or the psychologist requires as part of his training. It is of equally central relevance to other professions which also depend on it as a means of procuring information for specific purposes. The information obtained by the interview does not only consist of items of fact as this is usually understood, but could include data on the states of feeling, the mental attitudes and the emotional problems that are bound up with social living.

The social scientist, and all those whose professional interests are bound up with the lives of human beings in society, cannot be expected to obtain information by means of closely controlled experiments, since human beings do not lend themselves to experimentation as easily as inanimate objects do. The reasons why this is so have been discussed for decades, but they are still as relevant to contemporary society as they have always been in the past.

First, there are many ethical problems which could arise in the event of people being used as guinea-pigs for the purpose of obtaining information. For example, the social worker with an interest in the social problems associated with immigrant communities cannot be expected to expose members of such communities to different situations in order to discover their reactions; nor can the sociologist or the psychologist with a similar interest be expected to advocate a policy of mass migration of peoples in order to discover a range of information concerning their reactions to unfamiliar and stressful environments. The democratic values of Western society demand that the well-being of the individual be protected; they do not permit the use of human beings in experiments without regard to their safety and welfare.

Second, human beings cannot be assumed to be simply 'units' which do not interact with each other and which can therefore

be manipulated at will in experiments. Even if there were no fundamental ethical objections to their being used in experiments,
individuals would nevertheless interact with each other and thereby
frustrate attempts to draw simple conclusions. They possess attitudes, feeling and sympathy; they possess the faculty of thinking
and consciousness; they fall in and out of love. Their action, at any
one point in time, is influenced by motivational factors which are
within their personalities and cannot therefore be accounted for
in terms of external, mechanical forces. This distinguishes them
from inanimate physical objects which can be manipulated at will
in experiments, and makes it difficult to draw simple and straightforward conclusions, even if the fundamental ethical objections
to experimentation with human beings are set aside.

The interview, on the other hand, provides a framework of
activity which involves human beings. This framework makes it
possible to obtain information about human beings. Its use does
not run the danger of transgressing the fundamental ethical values
to which democratic societies subscribe, but often incorporates respect for them.

However, this does not mean that objections cannot be raised.
Many people object to being interviewed because they see the
activities involved as constituting an unwelcome intrusion into
their privacy; they see the interviewer as someone who seeks private and confidential information and whose primary interest is
to 'dabble his fingers in the stuff of other men's souls'. Objections
of this sort are commonly heard today and can make life difficult
for the social worker who is usually concerned to 'help' the client.

Such objections have to be understood in the light of the
greater exposure to interviewing which most people have experienced in the last two decades compared to earlier periods in history.
Opinion polls, such as the Gallup Poll, employ the interview on
an almost daily basis in order to discover people's views on many
problems of national importance. These problems range from the
advisability of a British nuclear test programme to the issue of
British entry into the European Economic Community. Market research organizations employ the interview to find out whether certain commercial products are preferred by the housewife as against
others. Social surveys take interviewing into the streets and are
widely used to find out people's views on issues as diverse as student
disturbances and government provision of milk for school children.
Such extensive use of the interview by various organizations has
meant that in the last two decades the average person has been
more exposed to the constituent activities involved than his counterpart in any earlier period in history. It is understandable, therefore,
that he should think of interviewing as an intrusion into his private

life. It is equally understandable that his wife should think of an interview as an unnecessary interruption of her daily routine in the home. Most interviewers are trained to recognize such objections and to adopt techniques which respect the privacy of the individual. Nevertheless, such objections will always be advanced, partly because of the greater exposure to interviewing which the average person experiences today and partly because the information requested will always impinge somewhat on the private lives of the respondents.

While such objections can never be lightly dismissed, they are not as fundamental as are the ethical objections to experimentation with human beings. They emphasize the need for the interviewer to respect the individuality of the client and to adopt those techniques which would highlight this. By respecting the individuality of the client, the democratic traditions of Western societies are reflected in the interview situation. This makes the interview a more acceptable means for obtaining information. It emphasizes the importance of gaining the confidence of the respondent by providing him with clear explanations of the nature of the information required and the purpose for which it is required. Where the interviewee is made to feel that the information requested, even if of a confidential nature, is for a specific purpose which might benefit him, his confidence in the interview is likely to be high.

Understanding the interview

Confidence is important, not only on the part of the respondent, who must be made to feel that the purpose of the interview is not to obtain information which would injure his interests, but also on the part of the interviewer whose skill can be crucial to the proceedings. The confidence with which an interviewer approaches an interview situation depends on the extent to which he is aware of the psychological and sociological implications of the interview, as well as the nature of the information which he seeks to obtain. Most interviewers find it easier to handle the latter than the former. The information required would either have been explained to him or he would, by virtue of his experience, be aware of the relationship which exists between the information he seeks and the problem areas of the life of the client which he would need to explore. But while he may be aware of the nature of the information required, he may not be as aware of the extent to which the psychological difficulties, mental state and attitudes of the client enter into the proceedings. His confidence in his own role would be higher where he is aware of both sets of factors.

The social worker is usually expected to be familiar with these two sets of factors, since his awareness of the relationship between the nature of the information which he requires and the problem areas in the lives of his clients is central to his 'caring' function. Yet it is because of this almost instant assumption of familiarity that interviewing is often allocated to peripheral sections of textbooks and training manuals in the social sciences in general. As a result, little attempt has been made to trace the relationship which exists between interviewing and communication in social work, even though the core of social work practice is heavily dependent on the art of interviewing and on communication.

This almost instant assumption of familiarity tends to reinforce the widespread, but false, impression that good interviewers are born, not made. According to this impression, skill in interviewing is an ability which is influenced by genetic factors in the personality.

This impression should not be taken seriously, for not only is it false but it also operates as a ready-made justification for ignoring the range of knowledge about interviewing which is now available, and for confirming the self-conception of the experienced practitioner of the art. It is perhaps natural that the experienced practitioner should wish to have his self-conception confirmed from time to time; nevertheless, the impression that good interviewers are helped along by genetic factors does more than to simply confirm the self-conception of the experienced practitioner: it reinforces the associated view that an interview is a matter which concerns only the two individuals who, in a personal interview, are physically involved in the encounter. This view is as over-simplified as the former 'congenital' view is false. The interview may require two individuals in a physical sense, but the social context within which they communicate with each other, the language and signs by which they undertake such communication and the cultural groupings in society from which they derive are all factors whose influence can be felt within the interview situation but are independent of the personalities of the participants.

The skills of interviewing which the experienced practitioner obtains by dint of diligent application and long years of service can be imparted to others. A wide range of knowledge is available on the complexities of interviewing which can be utilized by those who are less experienced. This knowledge has never been brought together and presented in a digestible form. Much of it remains hidden in the pages of technical journals which do not reach more than a small proportion of those who are professionally interested in the subject. The aim of this book is to present this knowledge in an easily comprehensible form and to show, thereby, that interviewing is far more complex than may have been supposed.

The interview touches on many aspects of human behaviour and communication; it mirrors the characteristics of the society within which interviewer and interviewee operate. It invokes linguistic symbols and psychological tensions; feelings which are deep-seated can be unearthed and can sometimes lead to violent outbursts of an uncontrollable kind. Our presentation of the manner in which these different sources of complexity and tension operate within the context of the interview situation, should emphasize the crucial role which the interview must continue to play, both in the diagnosis and in the treatment of social problems, particularly within the context of social work.

The professions which employ the interview are as numerous as are the contexts in which it is employed. These range from research in sociology and psychology through to medical practice and psychiatry, as well as many areas of social work. Such widespread use of the interview makes it difficult to entertain wide generalizations as to the human processes which can be involved. These processes are not invoked to the same degree in every context in which the interview is employed. For example, a market research interview dealing with a housewife's preference for a particular brand of coffee is unlikely significantly to affect her psychological constitution, whereas a psychiatric interview with the same client is more likely to do so. Wide generalizations concerning the extent of the intrusion of psychological crises and emotions cannot therefore be made without regard to the professional context within which the interview is employed. Nevertheless, such limited generalizations as can be made must be based on those common denominators which all interviews share.

Our discussion in the following pages is directed mainly to these common denominators for it is these which highlight the uniqueness of the interview as a means of obtaining information about human behaviour and problems. These denominators must be reflected in any definition of the interview, because they provide the foundation upon which limited generalizations about the interview can be based. How, then, can the interview be defined? This is a fundamental question which leads off into related questions such as : What are the common denominators which all interviews share? What are the general goals and objectives which are served by the interview? Are there different kinds of interviews? If so, by means of what criteria can distinctions be drawn between them? The answers to these questions all turn on the fundamental question of the definition of the interview.

The problem of definition: interviewing and counselling

Definitions often create more difficulties than they solve. On the one hand, they are usually judged to be adequate if they provide clarification of the issues as a point of departure for any discussion. The usefulness of definitions in this respect must therefore depend on the extent to which they provide precise identification of the phenomenon under consideration. Where that phenomenon is of a general character, is used in a wide range of contexts and professions, and has a long history behind it, as is the case with the interview, attempts to ensure precision in the description of its constituent components can often lead into complex debates as to which components are essential and which are peripheral. Further attempts to resolve such debates often result in a proliferation of 'operative terms' which might do justice to a dictionary. All too often, such 'operative terms' overwhelm the student. Far from providing clarification of issues, then, definitions can sometimes result in confusion.

However, it should be recognized that no definition can ever be so precise as to eliminate all controversy. There is certainly no widely held definition of the interview which adequately highlights its central characteristics, as well as the varying situations and contexts in which it is usually employed. The most that can be expected is a working definition of the interview which provides a brief but general conception of some of its important characteristics, which can be expected to occur in most situations and contexts in which it is employed. The definition that follows must therefore be seen as a working picture for the purposes of our discussion. It should serve to direct atttention to some of the important common denominators of the interview.

The most convenient starting point for any attempt at defining the interview is to be found in the recognition that, first, the activities which go on are aimed at facilitating communication. Communication in society occurs outside of the context of the interview as well as within it. What distinguishes the communication which goes on in the interview is that it has a specific goal, which is closely related to the objective of the interview, as against the general nature of communication in society at large. The recognition that the interview provides a means of communication which has a specific goal is fundamental to an understanding of how it operates.

Second, the interview is firmly rooted in society and is inconceivable outside of a social context. The wider implications of this for the activities which go on within the interview will be dealt with later on in the book. What should be stressed at this point is that it is a human activity. Interaction between the interviewer and interviewee is influenced by the social norms of the wider society within which it occurs. The form which communication takes within the interview situation is also determined by the wider society and is, to this extent, independent of the personalities of the participants. Human involvement in the interview is a second crucial characteristic of the interview.

A third and equally crucial characteristic is the fact that the interview is aimed at obtaining information. The nature of this information varies. It can include straightforward facts, as well as material on emotional reactions and psychological tragedies. This information may be aimed at improving the social worker's understanding of the client's problems where the interview occurs within the field of social work. It may also be aimed at presenting the client with material which allows him to gain insight into his own behaviour and its relationship to others. Sometimes, the information obtained will be useful for diagnosing the problems which the client experiences and will lead to the adoption of appropriate treatment procedures. On other occasions, the information obtained may be useful only for the facts it contains.

If the information obtained in an interview varies according to the specific objectives which that interview is designed to serve, its nature is usually determined prior to the encounter between interviewer and interviewee. Prior determination of the nature of such information is often necessary in order to relate the questions which will be asked to the specific objectives of the interview.

This does not mean that the information which is required of any interview can be predicted by the interviewer before the interview gets under way. The processes of communication which go on within the interview situation arise so spontaneously that prediction of the information which results is not possible. One of the perennial questions in the social sciences is concerned with the extent to which human behaviour can be predicted. We need not enter too far into this question in order to recognize that neither the products of the interaction of human beings nor the behaviour of any individual can be fully predicted as a general rule. Human interaction always involves unique and spontaneously produced elements which cannot be predicted.

The element of predetermination which characterizes the information content of an interview cannot be described by the term 'prediction' in the total sense which this term often conveys. What this element directs attention to is the fact that the broad outlines of the information required are usually envisaged before the actual encounter between the participants in an interview. In the actual course of that interview, these outlines are extended, elaborated and, indeed, changed. But it is because of this element of predetermination that control can be exercised over the flow of communication. The prior determination of these broad outlines is often referred to as the 'planning' aspect of the interview.

English and English (1958, p. 247) stressed these three elements in their description of the interview as 'a directed conversation with a person or persons that is designed to elicit certain predetermined kinds of information for the purposes of research or to aid in guidance, diagnosis or treatment'. However, these authors must have had in mind the use of the interview in those professional contexts in which research, guidance, diagnosis or treatment are important. The use of the interview is not confined to these contexts. It is also employed to obtain information of a factual nature. The tourist who engages a policeman in a protracted discussion of the nature of British society is interested in obtaining factual information out of personal interest. Any adequate definition must recognize this terminal use of the interview, as well as its more instrumental use in those professional contexts in which guidance, research, diagnosis and treatment are important.

Another definition by Brayfield (1950) demolishes the distinction between the act of communication and the information content of the interview by describing it simply as a 'vehicle for counselling'. However, this definition also oversimplifies the range of uses to which the interview can be put. Interviewing is used in those professional contexts in which counselling is important as well as in those contexts where this is not paramount. The term 'counselling' strongly connotes, first, an implicit intention to help those who are being counselled; second, it implies that the interest of those being counselled is a paramount consideration in the encounter. Third, it implies that the role of the counsellor is concerned with facilitating the adjustment of those who are being counselled. Accordingly, the term is often applied to the 'caring' professions such as social work and psychotherapy. Encounters between criminal suspects and the police can therefore not be described as 'counselling' whereas encounters between mental patients and social workers can be described as such. The term 'counselling' is most often used in America in the context of the work of the 'caring' professions.

By demolishing the distinction between the act of communication and the information content of the interview which we made before, Brayfield also implies that the term 'counselling' can be used interchangeably with the term 'interviewing'. This is true to a large extent in the context of social work and psychotherapy. For this reason, the term 'counselling' is most often used in social work and psychotherapy in America where 'interviewing' would be used in Britain. This is because these professions emphasize the need to relate subsequent activities to information concerning

8

the individual needs of the client. Medical and psychiatric practice also emphasize this diagnostic element.

Nevertheless, these terms are best used separately because not every interview encounter is equally closely tied in with diagnostic concerns, and to treat counselling and interviewing as interchangeable concepts could well lead to the erroneous impression that interviews either do not take place, or cannot exist, outside of the diagnostic concerns of the social worker or the psychotherapist; nor, indeed, do all interviews invoke the psychological characteristics of the participants to the same extent. The budding journalist, working for his school magazine, is neither interested in diagnosis nor in observing the psychological reactions of the headmaster to his questions. Similarly, the job interview which an applicant undergoes is far removed from counselling as the term is normally used in the 'caring' professions. Brayfield's description of the interview as a vehicle for counselling therefore amounts to a 'partial' description of the interview; it cannot be correctly applied to all interviews. Whereas some interviews are centrally concerned with counselling, others are not. In short, counselling always takes the form of an interview, but interviews need not necessarily be concerned with counselling.

Apart from the element of oversimplification in Brayfield's description of an interview, it should be clear from our discussion that the interview must possess a basic structure if communication is to be facilitated. This communication, to be sure, often takes the form of a conversation between two sets of persons, but clarity demands that we reserve the term 'conversation' for the ordinary usage which we normally give it. I can have a conversation with my local postman, my mother, my father and my children. Indeed, I can have a conversation with any one I care to speak to but this conversation has little, intrinsically, to do with the interview. A conversation, as such, is a reflection of the importance of communication to society in general and of the enduring nature of language.

If conversations occur within the interview situation, this is because the interview utilizes forms of commmunication which come from outside that setting. The danger of describing the communication which takes place in the interview as 'conversation' is two-fold. First, it under-emphasizes the specific nature of the communication and confuses it with what we normally do with our postmen, parents and children. It would be highly peculiar, indeed, if we were to describe the action of talking with our postmen, parents and children as interviewing. In line with its normal usage, we would normally refer to this activity as conversation.

9

Second, information is also transferred by non-verbal means in the interview situation, which the notion of 'conversation' fails to capture. Signs, gestures and facial expressions can often convey additional, and sometimes more significant, information than anything which can be expressed in words. Such non-verbal forms of communication can be more crucial where participants in an interview suffer from speech impairment. But even where speech is not impaired in any way, respondents may adopt stereotyped replies which conceal their personal involvement in the issues under consideration. For example, Taylor (1972) has shown that sex offenders brought before the courts often adopt stereotyped responses for their actions which relieve them of personal responsibility. 'I don't know what came over me' or 'I blacked out at the time' are stereotyped responses which such offenders employ to relieve themselves of their guilt. In such situations, non-verbal cues such as facial expressions and hand gestures can provide a means of getting through such responses. The social worker involved in comparable interview situations would wish to penetrate beyond such stereotyped responses.

The distinction between 'conversation' and communication in the context of the interview is therefore a real one which not only avoids confusion between our everyday activity and what goes on in the interview situation, but it also emphasizes the fact that more information can be communicated by non-verbal means than can be expressed in words, even though words and their linguistic rules remain important components of languages. Indeed, some writers stress both the verbal and non-verbal aspects of communication by referring to the former as the language of words and to the latter as body-language or the language of signs.

In sum, the conversation which takes place within the interview is of a specific character. Its specific character is determined by the two sets of persons who are involved in the act of communication, their relationships to each other both before and during the course of the interview, and the inherent assumptions which underlie the roles of interviewer and interviewee.

Definition of the interview

On the basis of the considerations advanced above, we can approach a working definition of the interview by describing it as a framework for communication which involves two sets of persons in an encounter whose primary objectives are usually related to the procurement of factual information, diagnosis and therapy. Interviewing is the human activity which takes place within the framework of communication inherent in the interview. In terms of this working definition, the interview can be regarded as a technical instrument which is concerned with communication, and its use can be evaluated in terms of the practical extent to which it enhances communication in specific contexts.

The roles of interviewer and interviewee

Prior determination of the broad outlines of the information content of an interview contributes towards the allocation of the roles of interviewer and interviewee. These roles have specific but vaguely understood meanings, according to Mayer and Timms (1970), for the participants. They involve expectations which are brought to the interview situation and are not products of that situation. They are social in origin and constitute part of the social context within which interviewing can be undertaken.

The social origin of roles and their attendant expectations will be discussed in further detail in the next chapter but a brief illustration of the way these role expectations operate can be seen in a doctor–patient interview. Both participants in this interview come to the encounter with certain expectations about each other. The expectation of the doctor in relation to the role of the patient is that the latter will be receptive to medical information, he will play a 'passive' role in the proceedings and will carry out the instructions and prescriptions that are made for him. The role of the doctor, in the mind of the patient, is that he will be skilful and confident in the execution of his medical duties, and will prescribe treatment in the light of the best interests of the patient. Where these expectations are not fulfilled, anxiety results on both sides. The anxiety of the patient might make his condition worse, while the anxiety of the doctor might interfere with the execution of his medical skills. The charge of 'quackery' or 'unethical' conduct in relation to the doctor's role points to a lack of fulfilment of the patient's expectations. Similarly, embarrassment in social interaction in general can be attributed, as Goffman does (1956), to a lack of fulfilment of the expectations which are held by the participants. These expectations are social in origin and exist, however unclearly, prior to the encounter.

The expectations which are attached to the roles of 'interviewer' and 'interviewee' are not only concerned with the skills which are adopted but often also involve a number of cultural variables that come from the wider society. Communication in the interview involves the use of language and dialect variations. Such variations characterize different social and cultural groups in the society. These variables can intrude into the proceedings and can influence the conduct of the participants as well as the information which is communicated. We shall examine the way in which these factors intrude into the interview in a later chapter.

The structure of the interview

Our working definition points to some of the common characteristics which all interviews share, irrespective of the immediate purpose for which they may be set up or the professional context within which they may be employed. This structure can be represented by a simple diagram as in Figure 1.

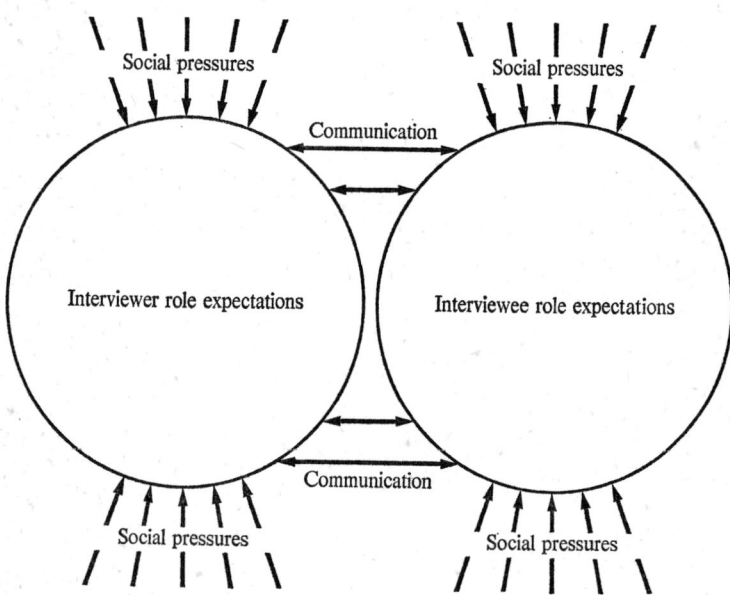

FIGURE 1 *The structure of the interview as a field of forces*

It consists of four features: first, the persons who are participating in the interview; second, the inherent role expectations which the participants attach to each other and which defines the obligations of each participant; third, the actual communication which takes place (represented by unbroken arrows in the centre of Figure 1) and, fourth, the social and cultural pressures acting on all participants which subtly pressure them to react in specific ways according to their cultural background (e.g. race, sex, social class, etc.). These four factors constitute the basic elements that go to form the structure of the interview and they are always present irrespective of the professional context within which the interview is employed.

An interview proceeds in three phases: the first phase or beginning, the second phase or the body of the interview, and the third phase or termination of the interview. These phases merge into each other as the interview progresses. Certain elements of skill are more appropriate to certain phases than others. For instance, skill elements which are focused on 'laying the bait' (to use a common American expression) tend to be focused on the first phase of the interview. We shall take up these skill elements in a later chapter.

The four structural elements outlined here are carried over all three phases of the interview and are in dynamic interaction with each other. At any one moment and in any phase, the social and cultural pressures might be emphasized relative to the others, whereas in another moment the communication content may be emphasized.

Nevertheless, these four elements represent the common denominators of all interviews. In view of these, an interview can be thought of as a complex of dynamic forces which constantly interact with each other as the interview progresses.

This description of the basic structure of an interview has been presented in a simplified form in the interest of clarity. It presumes that the roles of interviewer and interviewee always remain distinct throughout an interview, such that an interviewer cannot ever become the interviewee. In reality, however, the distinction between these two roles is not always so clear-cut. In some circumstances, the interviewee changes roles with the interviewer in the course of the same interview, as the communication ebbs or flows during the encounter.

Nevertheless, a complete transformation of the roles of interviewer and interviewee would lead to a breakdown of the interview and would considerably distort the results. This, in fact, is one of the characteristics of a bad interview. 'Turning the tables' on the interviewer is the best way to frustrate his efforts. However, most interviews involve a limited degree of role transfer between interviewer and interviewee, but this does not usually go so far as to completely destroy and frustrate the participants' expectations of each other's roles. A minimal degree of role separation between interviewer and interviewee remains essential to any interview. Certain skill elements employed by the interviewer can help to reinforce role allocation in the interview situation.

A much greater degree of interchange occurs outside the context of the interview since the social work interviewer, for example, can be an interviewee for a new job at one moment, or a medical or psychiatric patient at another moment. Society at large consists of diverse forms of interaction, each one of which requires some degree of role allocation. The social worker, in his capacity as a person in his own right, is involved in all these forms of interaction from one moment to the next, as father, local preacher, table-tennis player or motorist. The roles of interviewer and interviewee may be dropped from one moment to the next as he participates in different forms of social interaction. Indeed, he must 'drop one hat for another' during the course of interaction in everyday life. Such role transfers constitute a normal aspect of social interaction in the wider society. They constitute a generic framework of role allocation within which the transfer of roles between interviewer and interviewee can be seen as a specific example in the specific context of the interview.

The goals of the interview

Interviews serve a number of general goals which can be isolated for the purpose of our discussion. There are three such goals. The first is concerned with the procurement of information for the interviewer/social worker. The nature of this information will vary as we have suggested earlier, but the focus of the communication which takes place is on the client/interviewee. The role of the interviewer/social worker would therefore be largely concerned with adopting various skills by which communication from the client/interviewee could be enhanced. The client may well have requested the interview because he experiences problems which he is incapable of solving on his own. He therefore remains the focus of the activities which go on in the interview. It is his individual needs and problems which should be the paramount consideration. The interview, for him, provides an opportunity to discuss his problem and to 'tell it like it is'. It is his moment. The direction of communication is therefore from the interviewee or client to the interviewer or social worker.

A second goal of the interview is to provide information for the client. In this situation, the focus of the communication which takes place is on the social worker who has to provide information for the client. For example, workers in the Citizens' Advisory Service are often involved in interview situations in which they provide information for the client pertaining to welfare services and other facilities of which the client may be unaware. The social worker sometimes has to perform this service. Similarly, civil servants who administer Criminal Injuries Compensation or Old Age Insurance Schemes often have to provide information for clients. In all such cases, the burden of selecting the items of information which should be communicated to clients rests with the social worker or civil servant, for the focus of communication is on him.

In social work, this second goal is often combined with the first since information is often passed from interviewer to interviewee and vice versa within the same interview. In this sense, one can describe the information content of an interview as being the result of mutual exchange. However, care must be exercised in delineating the roles of interviewer and interviewee, for while any interview may be regarded as a 'joint quest' as Bogardus (1936) once described it, nevertheless the focus of communication differs in the first-mentioned situation as compared with the second. In the former, the 'spotlight' is on the client/interviewee whereas in the latter, it is on the social worker.

A third goal of the interview is concerned with providing therapy for the client. Such therapy would have been devised with the interests of the client in mind and would have been based on a thorough consideration of his individual needs. Often the therapy is aimed at influencing the attitude of the client to his own behaviour and to the behaviour of other people. Psychiatric practice exemplifies this goal to a greater extent than social work does, for psychiatric interviewing often involves a protracted process of manipulating the psychological make-up of the patient so as to bring about a change of behaviour and attitudes. The idea of psychological manipulation is often held to border on unethical behaviour and is often scornfully dismissed by liberal-minded people in the same way that brain-washing is dismissed. This is because the volition of the patient can so easily be abused. However, psychological manipulation in a therapeutic interview need not necessarily involve transgressing the rights of the individual. It may be argued, in any case, that a certain element of manipulation is always involved in any interview since the interviewer implicitly sets out to orient the mental apparatus of the interviewee in certain directions which would enhance communication. In this sense, it can be said that the diagnostic interview—sometimes referred to as the First Interview—which is aimed at providing some understanding of the range and complexity of the client's problems, is as manipulative as subsequent treatment interviews.

These three goals are often served by the interview. In some professional contexts, the therapeutic goal may be more important. Often the social work interview is therapeutic. However, this is not always the case, particularly where caseworkers interview each other. In other contexts, such as in job evaluation interviews, the therapeutic element is usually absent.

Types of interviews: personal and group interviews

There are different types of interviews even though all interviews share the same common denominators, as has been shown. These can be distinguished from each other on the basis of a number of criteria. What are these criteria?

Distinctions between different types of interviews can be made on the basis of the numbers of persons involved, the extent to which errors (in the sense of inaccurate information) result, and in the practical limitations which attend their use in particular situations. We have so far discussed the interview in terms of two sets of persons but have not specified the number of persons who can be involved in a set. The roles of interviewer and interviewee are incorporated in two sets of persons but these do not necessarily always involve a one person to one person encounter. It is often assumed that an interview requires only two persons, one occupying the role of the interviewer and the other occupying the role of the interviewee. Many point, in justification of this assumption, to interviewing in the press, television, and medical interviews. Nevertheless, to think of the interview only in terms of a person to person encounter is to under-emphasize the degree of variety which is possible.

The kind of interview in which two individuals occupy the roles of interviewer and interviewee respectively is usually referred to as the *personal* interview or the *face to face* interview. The personal interview is widely employed in many professional contexts and has been correctly described by Bogardus (1936, pp. 113-14) as the best technique for obtaining information which is not superficial and which penetrates to the core of the life of the individual and 'to those unconscious psychological forces that shape it'. Nevertheless, the personal interview is only one type.

Another type, which can be employed in the appropriate setting, is the *group interview*. The group interview involves one person occupying the role of the interviewer but the role of the interviewee is collectively incorporated in a number of persons who are assembled together. To be exhaustive, the opposite situation must also be considered where a group of persons occupy the role of interviewer and one person occupies the role of interviewee. This is not a situation compounded out of the personal interview since the group of persons occupying the role of the interviewer all operate simultaneously. This kind of interview is, for obvious reasons, often confined to special situations (in military intelligence work for instance) and is rather rare outside such situations. But it is nevertheless a variation of the group interview.

There are other types of interviews which are compounded

out of the personal interview such as the *panel interview* and the *mass interview*. These are compounds of the personal interview because one person, at any one moment during the course of the interview, would encounter one other person out of a fixed and unchanging number of interviewees, in a panel in the case of the former, or a mass of people spread out over a whole country in the case of the latter. Market research organizations, pressed for time or for detail (or, indeed, both) tend to employ these sub-types of interviews. In a mass interview, many individual interviewers tackle many equally individual interviewees within a specified period of time (e.g. 24 hours) all over the country. In the panel interview, one individual interviewer tackles one interviewee at a time, but restricts all possible interviewees to a predetermined panel of people. However, we need not concern ourselves with these sub-types since they are compounded out of the personal interview and represent variations on this theme.

Personal interviews can be distinguished from group interviews not only in terms of the numbers of persons who occupy the roles of interviewer and interviewee respectively, but also in terms of the opportunities for errors and the practical limitations to their use.

Group interviews cannot be employed where information of a relatively confidential nature is required; nor is it ever possible subsequently to disentangle individuals' own private opinions from 'conventional' opinions invoked by the presence of other people. People react, unconsciously, to group pressures, and their opinions, obtained in a group context, may only partly reflect their true state of mind. One can imagine how useless information on the sexual practices of married couples would be if such information were to be obtained by group interviews. The famous Kinsey Report (1948) on the sex life of American males and females would not have been possible if group interviews were the only type available. People in groups tend to 'swing' their opinions in order to appear 'normal' and 'conventional' and this limits the use of information so obtained. It would be surprising to discover people in a dictatorial country saying anything which reflected on the unpopularity of the dictator—a familiar example.

Errors from this source are not necessarily confined to group interviews, but could also arise in personal interviews. Many studies in America have shown that negro interviewers tend to evoke one kind of response from negro interviewees on matters pertaining to internal politics, as against that evoked by white interviewers. To refer to this source of error in the context of group interviews is not to suggest that the same source of error cannot arise in personal interviews but to stress that group interviews provide

17

a much greater opportunity for this source of error to arise and to influence the information which is obtained. This tendency to reflect conventional opinions is often referred to as Social Desirability Motivation.

The greater possibility for error in group interviews restricts their use. They are often used to provide outline information which helps the interviewer to begin to explore the wider ramifications of the subject area in which he is interested. Accordingly, a social worker may use the group interview in order to find out, for example, the general views of young mothers as to whether school milk should or should not be provided for their children by the State. But the information thus obtained would be a poor indicator of their personal views as to whether they agree or disagree with the political decision to withdraw the free supply of milk to school children. Indeed, group interviews may well show that young mothers are opposed to the withdrawal of this service whereas subsequent personal interviews with them might well show the very opposite. The interviewer who is interested in personal and confidential information, would therefore either not use the group interview at all or might use it at the very beginning of his explorations into a subject area but follow it up with personal interviews.

Similarly, there is a range of professional contexts in which the group interview is not usually employed. In all those contexts where diagnosis and treatment are relevant, group interviews would be meaningless. Berg's (1955, Ch. 17) interview with a psychiatric patient who was afraid to marry could only have been undertaken by means of personal interviews, as could Morrissey's (1953) with children facing imminent death from congenital diseases.

There are other factors which set group interviews apart from personal interviews. Since group interviews make it possible for a collection of people who probably know something about each other to be interviewed in each other's presence, they tend to be less expensive than personal interviews. The personal interview might involve frequent calls by the interviewer and a considerable amount of probing during the interview. In those circumstances where penetrating information is required, more than one interview may be necessary and each interview might disintegrate in midstream where the proceedings touch on very sensitive issues. As will be shown in the following chapters, a personal interview is not just a physical encounter but also brings out the psychological tensions which both the interviewer and the interviewee experience in their daily lives. Berg (1955, p. 32) actually goes so far as to describe every interview as a psychological confrontation between two different personalities. We need not go this far in order to appreciate that the psychological functioning of individuals can be involved in the interview and can facilitate or impede the flow of communication by invoking anxieties and tension. For this reason, personal interviews tend to involve a greater expenditure of time, effort and, where appropriate, money, as against group interviews.

Group interviews also have another advantage which is not so obvious. This is wholly dependent on the nature of the group to be interviewed. Whenever such interviews are organized with groups which are homogeneous in many respects, persons with deep and specialized knowledge of the subject can be unearthed much more quickly than would be the case with personal interviews. In such interviews, persons within the group soon realize the limitations in their own knowledge and the existence of other people who are much more knowledgeable. One person with limited knowledge might make a statement on a subject which is then challenged by someone else with more knowledge within the group, thus forcing the former to defend himself and thereby display the full extent of his ignorance.

Young children tend to react far more readily to this kind of pressure than do adults and are therefore more suited to group interviews. This is because they do not possess sufficient experience and knowledge of facts to be completely adamant about their statements in a group setting. They are also less likely, for the same reason, to express a strong psychological compulsion to suppress or conceal their true states of mind and feeling. Adults, on the other hand, with a much more fully developed 'reserve mechanism' are more often under a compulsion to conceal even the most widely known triviality of man's existence, for psychological reasons. Group interviews therefore tend to be more successful when children in groups are involved. Indeed, Bogardus (1936, p. 110) carried out a number of successful interviews with groups of young boys by getting them to freely 'tell on each other', as each boy tried to counter challenges to his range of knowledge.

Persons with specialized knowledge who are revealed by group interviews can then be subsequently interviewed in personal interviews with much profit. But whether or not such persons would emerge would depend on the extent to which relationships within the group facilitate the breakdown of 'reserve mechanisms'. In other words, it cannot be asserted that these mechanisms can be broken down only in group interviews, since a satisfactory relationship between interviewer and interviewee in a personal interview could also achieve the same results. What can be said, however, is that such 'reserve mechanisms' can be more quickly broken down in group interviews than in personal interviews. This tendency for people to be pressured by the group is described by Allport (1962) as 'social facilitation'.

These considerations provide a basis on which distinctions between types of interviews can be made. They also indicate that the decision as to whether to employ a personal or a group interview in any situation is one which has to be taken on practical grounds. It is specific considerations such as these which are crucial in determining which type of interview should be undertaken.

They are also important in deciding whether sub-types of the personal interview such as *panel interviewing* or *mass interviewing* or sub-types of the group interview such as *joint interviewing* and *family interviewing* would be appropriate. Joint interviewing is often used in marriage counselling, with husbands and wives being interviewed simultaneously. Ehrenkranz (1967) has shown how successful such interviewing can be in marriage counselling. Family interviewing is a much more recent development and has been used in America in cases where there are multiple problems within one family, e.g. father is an alcoholic, mother a prostitute and children have criminal tendencies, etc. Jordan (1972, Ch. 4) has recently shown how useful joint interviewing can be in the context of problem families in his description of the Sharp family. However, family interviewing has yet to be fully applied to social work in England. Its attendant techniques have yet to be fully worked out. In the following chapters, we shall be most concerned with the personal interview since this is most widely adopted in most professional contexts, though some of the points that are discussed would also apply to the other types of interviews which we have discussed here.

The scope and organization of the book

This book is addressed primarily to the increasing numbers of students of social work whose needs are becoming more pressing as the scope of social work in contemporary society becomes progressively widened and as the degree of professionalism within social work increases. Its broad aim is to provide the student with as brief a coverage as possible of the available information on the subject of interviewing and its relationship to communication.

Human communication has received much attention from specialists in various disciplines which are only marginally, if at all, related to the sphere of social work. Accordingly, research work has been undertaken on human communication in psychology, sociology and, indeed, in physics, where communication goes far beyond the range of human beings into the wider arena of mechanical devices aimed at improving the transmission of information. This research took its point of departure from the basic recognition that human communication is central to social life, irrespective of the uses to which it might be put. In their attempt to understand human communication, all these disciplines have analysed and re-analysed various aspects of the subject.

Communication for the social worker takes place in the context of the interview. The interview therefore represents, for the social worker, one of the most important instruments by which his work can be undertaken, whether in the fields of educational guidance, psychotherapy or family casework. But while this connection between communication and interviewing might appear obvious in the form in which it is stated, nevertheless, little attempt has been made to trace the full extent of their interrelationship and to show the extent to which limitations in the former can interfere with the latter, and thus frustrate the efforts of the social worker in carrying out the 'caring' function which was always prominent in the development of social work.

In the chapters which follow, we present the material in such a way that the interests of both the social work student and those of the experienced practitioner whose interests lie outside social work, are catered for. The layout adopted should permit easy reference to specific aspects of interviewing and communication. Technical language forms an indispensable part of the material available. Nevertheless, we have endeavoured to explain such technical terms in every instance where a more familiar and less technical substitute could not be used in the interest of clarity. In general, however, we have attempted to minimize the use of such terms as far as possible. Where such terms as remain are intrinsically connected with experiments, minute details of these experiments have been dispensed with; only the bare outlines of such experiments are included.

Undoubtedly, this approach, as well as the method of presentation, reflects not only the instructional nature of the book but also the fact that the authors are involved in the teaching of degree students and professional social workers and are familiar with the particular requirements of those who will have cause to make the most use of the material presented.

In the chapters which follow, various aspects of the interview are examined within the framework of the definition that has been outlined in this chapter. Communication within the interview takes place against a background of social norms and values. Indeed, the whole fabric of society is reflected in the basic structure of the interview and regulate the relationships which arise. It provides the social context within which interviews occur and influences the nature of the information which is obtained, as well as the expectations and conduct of the participants. This context is examined in the next chapter.

The third chapter examines some of the cultural factors which have been shown to contribute a concrete effect on the reactions of interviewers and interviewees and on the proceedings of the interview.

Communication in the interview is facilitated in part by the use of language. However, language usage varies between communities and can introduce pressures into the proceedings of an interview. The way in which linguistic symbols are used by different groups in relation to interviewing and communication is dealt with in the fourth chapter.

But while the use of language facilitates communication, much more is communicated by non-verbal means. These non-verbal forms of communication are not peripheral to the information that is obtained, but form an integral part of it in many professional contexts, including that of social work. In some circumstances, they play a much greater part in the proceedings of the interview than might be supposed. These are discussed in detail in the fifth chapter.

Chapters 6 through to Chapter 9 are concerned with the technical aspects of the interview. The interview is a technical instrument which can be examined as such. Its technical usefulness turns on the skill with which it is used. These chapters discuss matters pertaining to the practical skills by which the interview can be undertaken.

The whole book is integrated in such a way that ideas introduced in one chapter are followed through and developed in subsequent chapters. The last chapter summarizes the salient considerations which are advanced in the earlier chapters. In general, the first five chapters deal with theoretical issues while the rest of the book presents practical considerations pertaining to interviewing and communication.

2

The social context of the interview

In the last chapter, we emphasized the importance of the interview in social work in particular and the role of communication in that connection. Our definition of the interview presents it as a form of communication which involves two sets of persons in an encounter whose primary objective is the procurement of information, the outlines of which are determined prior to the encounter. In elaborating on this definition, we stressed that the expectations of the roles of interviewer and interviewee derive from the wider society. In this chapter we are concerned to examine the nature of these expectations and the social pressures which influence the encounter of the participants.

Social interaction in the interview

The participants involved in an interview engage in social interaction during the course of that encounter. This interaction is not generically different from the social interaction which normally obtains in society. On the contrary, it represents one form into which social interaction can be incorporated. It is therefore necessary to examine social interaction in the wider society as a first step towards an understanding of its operation within the interview situation. It is through this interaction that the characteristics of the wider society are introduced into what might otherwise appear to be a unique encounter between interviewer and interviewee.

It is easy to assume that the interviewer and the interviewee are unique individuals who enter into the interview situation. Nevertheless, socialization forces them to bear the stamp of the society within which they have grown up and to take its characteristics into the interview with them. They therefore represent the agents by which the intrusion of the wider society into the interview situation is effected. In this sense, they do not stand as isolates in the interview situation.

The contrast with a Robinson Crusoe situation is the most obvious one which can be raised here, for it is often assumed that when Robinson Crusoe went to his desert island home he left the characteristics of his Scottish homeland behind him. In fact, he could not have avoided taking these characteristics to the desert island because he grew up in Scotland and had, as a consequence, inculcated the norms that are contained within that society without knowing it. Robinson Crusoe was therefore as much of a Scotsman in his desert island home, as were the many other Scotsmen whom he presumably left behind.

Since social interaction takes place within the interview situation, an understanding of its operation within that context can only be obtained by examining the components of social interaction which obtain in the wider society.

The components of social interaction

An interview is undoubtedly a human situation, not only in the sense that human beings occupy the roles of interviewer and interviewee but also in the sense that both persons are 'forced' to interact with each other. This interaction is influenced by the wider society in so far as the participants conform to certain *basic norms* concerning how people behave in public, how people avoid being impolite, and every other 'norm' concerning the behaviour of people towards each other which one acquires during the process of growing up. For this reason, it can be argued that an interview is a phenomenon which requires the existence of society and cannot therefore exist outside a social setting. These basic norms are brought into the interview by the participants and regulate their actions and reactions towards each other without the participants necessarily being aware of it. It is these norms which regulate social interaction generally.

These norms constitute one important component of social interaction in general, and regulate the behaviour of individuals in every setting in which they might find themselves. They are of a general nature in the sense that they form part of the background of the structure of society within which the individual is socialized. It is their imperceptible inculcation into the growing child which makes the child 'social'.

In the course of socialization, the child is taught to respect his elders and to accord respect to special persons within the community such as his teachers or his parents. He also comes to learn that there are a number of roles in the world outside the immediate family circle which impose certain obligations on the persons who occupy them on the one hand, and demand his respect on the other. Accordingly, the role of the King gradually comes to possess a certain intrinsic meaning for the child; he comes to recognize that one behaves in a certain way towards a king.

However, the growing child does not learn only about the role obligations attendant on important personalities such as kings and prime ministers; these roles are very specific. He also comes to recognize that there are many other roles in society and that these all have obligations as well as rights. Many of these roles are general and are not confined to any particular category of persons. The roles of interviewer and interviewee, for instance, as so general that anyone can occupy them from time to time.

There are many other roles, of an equally general nature, whose existence does not enter into the conscious thought of the individual until he 'wears' them. Nevertheless, he is usually aware of the obligations that are attached to social roles, however vague this awareness may be. His understanding of the obligations attached to such roles is not dependent on the fact of his having occupied them; if this were not so the role of an 'astronaut', for instance, would remain incomprehensible to everyone except those who have actually been placed in this position. On the contrary, the individual's understanding of the obligations attached to a role is of a general nature and is learned through the process of socialization. This understanding does not depend on the fact of his having occupied such a role.

The obligations that are attached to any role are based on the basic norms of society. Both the norms and the various role obligations which are learnt during the process of socialization become second nature to the growing child and thereby become an unconscious aspect of his existence. They thus come to exert an important influence, not only on his public behaviour, as Goffman (1963) has so carefully demonstrated, but also on his behaviour with members of his own family circle. They prescribe 'correct' behaviour and proscribe 'incorrect' behaviour. They determine and regulate behaviour which is appropriate to one's sex or social status.

These norms are not created by individuals but form part of the web of social structure into which the individual is born. For this reason, the death of any particular group or generation of people does not affect their importance for the functioning of society. It is by the permanence of these norms, as well as by the fact that individuals who are socialized into them never come to be fully conscious of their influence, that stability and continuity in society is made possible. They are, to this extent, crucial for social interaction in general, irrespective of whether this occurs within the interview situation or outside it.

These norms are not restricted to any one society but are found in all societies. Their content may be influenced by the particular cultural context within which they are found and may, for this reason, appear to differ appreciably between different societies. For example, one of the important norms which the growing child in Europe learns is that of respect for parents. This same norm is also taught in China. The average child in China is equally aware of its importance because he will have been socialized into an unconscious compliance with this norm. His actions will be regulated by this norm since he will, like his European counterpart, see respect for parents as being a 'good' thing.

Nevertheless, the European child will also have been socialized into the recognition that parental respect is not all that is important and that respect for the individuality of people is equally important. The Chinese child, on the other hand, will have been socialized into believing that parental respect represents the highest positive value (in so far as the religion of Confucianism stresses this) and cannot be 'check-mated' by any other norm. The result, as shown by Lang (1946), is that the Chinese child lives through a relatively dictatorial and oppressive regime in which every older person within the family exercises strong control over him.

However, such differences between the norms of different societies rest on a common core of universal ideas which all societies share in common, such as, for example, the universal injunction against the murder of one's compatriots. This is not to say that different societies do not have fundamental cultural differences in their attitudes to magic, religion, etc.; rather, it suggests that the cultural differences which are exhibited by different societies do not exclude the existence of a common and universal core of ideas concerning how to behave in public, how to deal with persons in authority, and so on. These ideas are incorporated into the norms of every society. These norms, general and unconscious as they might appear to be, nevertheless constitute an important component of social interaction in general. Accordingly, their influence will be felt in all the numerous forms which social interaction takes, such as the interview situation.

A second component of social interaction concerns the *specific values* associated with specific roles such as doctors, professors, clergymen and so on. These values are superimposed on the basic norms of society and tend to be much nearer to the consciousness of the individual. They are specific in the sense that they are important for the execution of the obligations attached to any particular role. For example, one of the central values of the medical profession is that the practitioner turns out at any time to heal his patients, never, of course, to kill them. The idea of selfless devotion to the service of healing the sick is an important professional value which is central to the role of being a doctor. It is specific to doctors and medical workers, but not to other professional groups unrelated to the medical field. These other professional groups also have values which are equally specific to their professional practices, even if these values are not formally embodied in a disciplinary code as is the case with doctors and the General Medical Council in Britain.

However, specific values are not always associated with the professions, though their specific nature is probably best indicated in this connection. They can also be related to specific groups of people such as a class of warriors—the feudal knight in Europe with his code of chivalry or the Samurai warrior in Japan with his code of behaviour—or to an immigrant group. The Sikh, for instance, attaches a specific religious value to his hair and symbolizes this by wearing a particular kind of headgear. The significance of such specific values is often taken for granted by such groups, just as much as doctors take their specific obligation to heal the sick for granted, but they are nevertheless important values which regulate their social interaction with other people and with each other. Specific values, such as these, are usually raised into sharp relief where the categories of people to whom these values are specific move into unfamiliar situations, as in the case of medical doctors in Nazi Germany who were forced to carry out dangerous experiments on prisoners during the Second World War, or Sikh bus conductors who were once faced with the request that they wear regulation caps.

The result of the superimposition of specific values on the norms of society is that the incumbents of roles are expected, first, to conduct themselves according to the basic principles concerning polite behaviour which apply to everyone, as well as, second, to respect the dictates of the specific values which apply to their own particular categories. Accordingly, the Sikh is expected to conduct himself with politeness and decorum, as well as to respect the specific and traditional dictates of his religious affiliation. Similarly, the medical doctor is expected to conduct himself according to the basic norms governing polite behaviour as well as to execute his medical functions with due regard to the ethics of the professional group to which he belongs.

These two components of social interaction are closely related to each other. The basic norms provide the foundation on the basis of which specific values can be added in later life. The two have been separately treated in our discussion in order to show that norms are simple—how to behave in public for instance—and values are specific—such as the code of confidentiality among doctors. Both components enter into the interview situation through the interviewer and the interviewee. They derive from the wider society. Once taken into the interview situation, they exert their influence on the proceedings which take place.

A third component of interaction can be described as *social orientation* (as against the more confusing term of value-orientation suggested by Parsons (p. 409) in 1951). Social orientation refers to the state of mind within the individual which 'forces' him to act according to the dictates of norms and specific values. As an orientation, it invokes the feeling states of the individual and directs them towards behaviour which is in keeping with the norms of society and the specific values which are appropriate to particular roles. It is a conception in the mind of the person which invokes his psychological constitution and creates a state of readiness to act in conformity with the norms and values of society. It is because of this conception, that the norms and specific values come to appear to the individual, not as legal injunctions created by an external agent which he is forced to obey, but as products of his own internal self. For this reason, contravention of these norms and values will certainly not bring down some law on one's head but would rather, and much more subtly, create a feeling of discomfort, shame or embarrassment. Social orientations, in this way, invoke the conscience or the super-ego (as Freud called it) and motivate the individual towards conformity.

This third component of interaction, like the other two mentioned, regulates social interaction in general and is taken into the interview situation by the participants. How, then, do they come to constitute the social context within which the interview can be conducted? How do they come to form the social framework of the interview?

The social framework of the interview

As a result of the operation of norms, specific values and social orientations, participants in the interview come to hold minimum expectations about each other's behaviour. They come to expect that each person will act in conformity with the norms of society and will therefore react politely and agreeably, even where he may not have met the other participant before. The exchange of salutations and the introductions that are normally made and taken for granted, constitute forms of action which derive from the wider society, but which form part of the shared expectations which participants come to the interview with. They rest on the basic norms of the society into which the participants would have been socialized.

These expectations are shared by the participants in the interview but do not normally enter into their conscious thoughts unless, that is, the behaviour of interviewer and interviewee contravenes them. Just as the norms that influence social interaction remain below the consciousness of people, so do these shared expectations which derive from them. They are nevertheless important in regulating the social interaction into which interviewer and interviewee enter when the interview is set in motion.

They regulate social interaction by 'altering' the individual's actions in a social direction. As Weber (1970) showed, the action of one person in relation to another is not necessarily a social action, but can be the product of involuntary reflex. For example, it is easy to conceive of a cyclist hitting a pedestrian and injuring him. Such action is not social. An action becomes social only to the extent that one recognizes that another person is involved. This recognition plays a part in determining the course of that action.

In practice, two individuals engaged in social interaction would each hold expectations about the behaviour of the other. Only where action is related to these expectations can one describe it as 'social'. A social action requires this element of 'directedness to others'. In terms of our earlier example, the cyclist who hits the pedestrian and injures him is certainly not involved in a social action, in so far as his action could not have taken existence of the particular pedestrian into account. In fact, we usually refer to actions which result in unintended consequences as 'accidents'. What, then, if he had deliberately wanted to kill the pedestrian?

In that case, his action would certainly not be described as 'social' because he would have taken the existence of the pedestrian into account in a negative way and his action would have fallen short of the expectations which the pedestrian held of him. The element of shared expectations which Weber stressed would not have been present and the negative value which the cyclist attached to the existence of the pedestrian would, indeed, qualify his action as being 'anti-social'.

In the context of the interview, the element of shared expectations between the participants would be present because they derive from norms, specific values and social orientations. Interaction in the interview demands that participants take each other's existence into account. The social interaction that takes place in that context therefore reflects the participants' possession of this element of shared expectations. It is in this way that the actions of interviewer and interviewee are constrained and regulated to conform to the widely accepted forms of behaviour which operate in the wider society.

These expectations are *minimal* expectations which derive from the wider society and are not directly related to the idiosyncracies of the individuals who are participating in the interview. The identities of the individuals who participate in the interview may change: they may be immigrants, fathers, skilled technicians, highly educated. Nevertheless, these minimal expectations are always present in the interview whenever two individuals encounter each other.

There are other expectations which are closely related to the idiosyncracies of the individuals who may be involved in the interview, such as their level of education, their sex, their social class, background etc., and these can play a relatively major role in the proceedings. Mayer and Timms (1970) have shown that these factors not only influence the proceedings of social casework interviews but can also determine whether or not clients express satisfaction or dissatisfaction with their encounters with social workers. We shall examine the role which such *major* expectations can play in the interview in some detail in the next chapter.

In sum, both the minimal and major expectations arise from social interaction in the wider society, and are involved in the interview. The identities of the participants are relatively unimportant since these expectations constitute a social framework within which any individual, irrespective of colour, creed, race or class, would operate in an interview. In providing a social framework for the actions of participants, they influence and determine the range of 'permissible' behaviour. The basic niceties which are found in social interaction in the wider society therefore come to be expected by both sets of participants in the interview as a matter of course, and without qualification or conscious thought. These expectations require that the widely accepted forms of introduction and salutation be exchanged within the interview situation. They ensure that an interviewer and an interviewee who have never seen each other before do not, nevertheless, salute each other with punches on the nose. It is because of their intrusion into the interview situation that one can assert that the interview cannot exist outside of society. It is inconceivable in any but a social context.

Time duration as a factor in the interview

The matter of time duration is one which is often raised in connection with the interview. It is often presumed that the social character of the interview, as well as the nature of information which is procured, depends on the length of time for which the interview is allowed to run. It is easy to understand this presumption since the average social worker is faced with a rather tight schedule in the course of his work and may well feel that his usefulness in supporting his client must be restricted by the fact that he can allow only a specified period of time for each case. In the face of this consideration, time comes to possess a value, since the amount of time which can be spent on any individual interview must remain restricted. The presumption that shortage of time must restrict the operation of those social elements which have been discussed above, as well as the worker's own usefulness in the interview, is therefore both a reflection of the latter's conscientiousness and of the administrative and other constraints within which he has to operate. It is as well, therefore, to be clear as to the influence of time duration on the interview, without minimizing its constraining influence in social work in general.

Time is of little significance as far as the shared expectations which we have discussed above are concerned. These expectations derive, in the last resort, from the basic norms which guide social interaction. The interview situation is one in which social interaction between interviewer and interviewee takes place and the participants approach it with these expectations. Even in the case of major expectations, such as those resulting from social class, sex, and educational level, time remains unimportant since these expectations intrude into short contact interviews as well as interviews of longer duration. Similarly, the development of supportive relationships in casework can be accomplished in short contact interviews, as well as in longer interviews, as Ferard and Hunnybun (1962, pp. 42-4) have emphasized. It is clearly not time, in itself, which is crucial for the social character of the interview, but other factors pertaining to the participants before the interview is set in motion, e.g. the amount of prior information available, the degree of sympathetic understanding which the social worker possesses before the interview commences, etc.

Time duration is equally unimportant in relation to the nature of the information which is obtained from an interview. The passage of time might increase the volume of communication between the participants, either in the sense that they talk a lot more to each other or in the sense that a wider range of non-verbal signs such as gestures, expressions, etc., are exchanged. But the passage of time by itself does not affect the amount of pertinent information which results from communication. This can be clearly seen in a schematic representation of the flow of human communication in two contrasting situations as provided in Figure 2.

In the first situation, two friends are communicating with each other. In the course of that communication a range of information (represented by dots) is exchanged. In the normal course of that communication, much would be said about a variety of things which do not have the slightest relevance for a diagnosis of the

Situation 1: Communication between friends

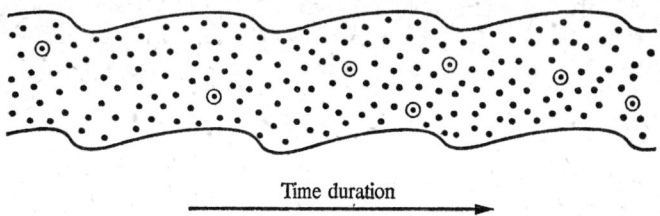

Time duration

Situation 2: Communication between client and social worker

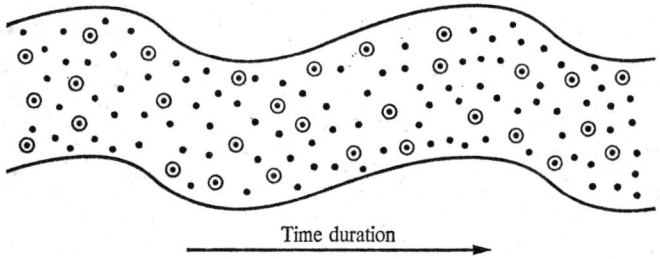

Time duration

FIGURE 2 *The flow of communication in two contrasting situations* (adapted from Kahn and Cannell, 1957)

needs of either one of the two participants. In the second situation in which the communication is more specifically concerned with an interview between a social worker and his client, the interview situation would compress the amount of relevant information (the ringed dots) into smaller time segments, according to the skill of the interviewer/social worker. The amount of pertinent information for social work diagnosis differs in both situations per time segment. If the second situation were to degenerate into the first, then the amount of pertinent information which the social worker would obtain in that situation would be correspondingly reduced.

It is very tempting to assume that more pertinent information can be obtained from an interview the longer the interview is allowed to go on. The amount of information that a skilled interviewer can obtain from any given interview is quite high *vis-à-vis* an unskilled interviewer in the same period of time. To drag out that same interview over a longer period of time could well prove counter-productive. Indeed, most interviews have a theoretical time limit after which continuation becomes counter-productive and results in diminishing returns. That limit cannot be subjected to generalization over all interviews irrespective of the professional context in which they occur, but varies with such contexts.

However, while time duration is of little importance to the operation of the social characteristics which we have discussed and to the amount of pertinent information which is obtained in an interview, there are nevertheless situations in which it can act as a 'helping' factor of some importance. In those situations where the information required is deeply concealed within the unconscious of the client, as in a psychiatric interview, for example, interviews of short duration would not be very useful. In such situations, an artificial restriction of interviewing time to the shortest period possible would not produce much information; neither would continuous extension of interviewing time necessarily produce more pertinent information.

Similarly, in social casework, interviews about problems which involve considerable tension in the mind of the client usually require a greater time duration than would be required in television interviewing, in which the information which is required usually concerns only impressions and opinions. An understanding of short-contact interviews, as they are called (Reynolds, 1932, and Young, 1935), and the circumstances in which they are best employed, is more important than a concentration on time by itself. Interviews which are artificially prolonged can lead to attention being shifted to interesting but irrelevant information in certain situations. Mayer and Timms (1970, p. 157) have shown that a failure to comprehend the role obligations of the social worker by working class clients tends to result in undue emphasis being placed by these clients on the friendliness or otherwise of casework agencies and their workers. Prolonged interviewing can increase this kind of emphasis on friendliness to the detriment of the objective goal of the interview.

In effect, time could provide a 'helping' factor in the interview situation but the extent to which it can play this role depends on the nature of the information required, the professional context of the interview and variable factors such as these.

Social work values in the interview

A further point which requires elaboration concerns the reflection of specific values on the activities of participants in an interview. We have shown above that specific values are based on norms and derive from the wider society; they are not intrinsic to the interview but are brought into it by the participants. Much has been

33

written about the specific values associated with social work, medical practice, and science in general. Indeed, a perennial debate has gone on for a decade at least concerning the social responsibilities of social workers, doctors and scientists. It was the scientists, specifically, who were quick to express their disillusionment with the service to which their work on the A-bomb was likely to be put in the future and raised the now important question of the responsibility of the scientist. The debate about the values of various professions was the outcome of that disillusionment.

The specific values of various professions reflect the bases on which their claim to be socially responsible can be based. For this reason, the development of consensus concerning values by any group of skilled workers is often taken to be a sign of professionalization. The transformation of this consensus into a disciplinary code is an indication of the degree of professionalization which has been attained. Accordingly, all professional bodies sooner or later come to enshrine a set of codes in their 'charters' designed to reflect those values to which their practitioners subscribe.

Wilensky and Lebaux (1958) have shown that signs of professionalization among social workers were evident since the 1950s. Nevertheless, professionalization made giant strides among social workers in Britain only during the course of the past decade and culminated in the creation, in 1970, of the British Association of Social Workers comparable to the National Association of Social Workers in America, which had a longer pedigree.

Not all social workers approve of the trend towards professionalization symbolized by the British Association of Social Workers. Some of them fear, as Heraud (1970) shows, that a degree of rigidity will be imposed on the social workers' activities and will be followed by a disciplinary code of ethics which may be rigidly enforced. Others feel that the co-ordination and unification of social work services which such a trend necessitates might well lead to a loss of meaningful contact with the wider community outside of the profession of social work. Despite these fears, the trend towards the professionalization of social work is likely to continue and the range of values to which social workers subscribe will, as a consequence, become more widely known and accepted by the community at large.

Now, the interview is a technical instrument for obtaining information and does not possess any values that are intrinsic to it. It can be used for social or anti-social purposes. In this sense, it can be considered to be analogous to the technical instruments which a scientist or medical practitioner uses. A thermometer, in this analogy, has no intrinsic connection with values and can be used as adequately by a Roman Catholic doctor opposed to abortion as by another with a different confessional affiliation. An interview is, by no means, a concrete technical instrument but its use is equally independent of values.

Nevertheless, its use can reflect the dominant ethical values of any professional group which employs it. A medical practitioner who employs the interview finds himself confronted, in that situation, with the code of values espoused by all doctors and the British Medical Association. A psychiatrist who employs hypnosis in an interview with a female patient may also find himself confronted by those values. They impose limitations on the kinds of behaviour which are considered to be permissible, because social interaction is involved in the interview. Such values are related to those which obtain in the wider society and serve to protect the public and the practitioner, by creating shared expectations on the one hand and by ensuring that actual behaviour conforms to such prior expectations on the other.

The values associated with the profession of social work are not as widely known and accepted by the general community as are the values associated with medical practice; nor is there anything but a limited consensus among social workers as to the values which should be considered to be central to their profession, as Timms (1970) has shown. Nevertheless, the client's right to self-determination and the voluntary nature of his demand for help is one value which few social workers would find objectionable. Respect for the dignity and self-respect of the client, and the latter's presumed possession of potentialities for managing his own life, are other values which few social workers would find objectionable. These values are all closely connected with a dominant respect for the individuality of the person, which is so important in the democratic way of life. Even the 'charitable impulse' which considerably influenced the development of social work in the USA and in Britain, and which some social workers now feel should be de-emphasized, was nevertheless closely related to the values of these societies in the nineteenth century, as Timms (1970), Salomon (1967), Emmet *et al.* (in Younghusband, 1967), Young and Ashton (1956) and Woodroofe (1962), among others, have shown. The use of the interview in social work must therefore correspondingly reflect these values.

If the trend towards professionalization among social workers in Britain continues and leads to the creation and imposition of a code of conduct, then the social worker who undertakes an interview might sooner or later recognize the intrusion of his professional values during the course of an interview since the notion of 'professional misconduct' would then become as valid as it is in medical practice today. Such a possibility is, at the moment, far-fetched and hypothetical. But though hypothetical, it nevertheless highlights the extent to which the specific values of the social worker and the values of the wider society can be reflected in the interview situation.

These considerations demand that the definition of the interview presented in the last chapter be amplified to include this reflective quality. It can be asserted, accordingly, that the interview is an act of communication between two sets of persons and is designed to elicit information but, in its operation, tends to reflect the dominant and specific values of the professional context within which it is employed and, through this, the values of the wider society. In itself, however, it remains a technical instrument which is potentially neutral.

Philosophical traditions

This tendency for interviewing to reflect the values and assumptions of the professions which employ it has resulted in the emergence of a number of different traditions. These traditions contain implicit philosophical conceptions about the nature of the human personality, some of which are derived from the mainstreams of Western philosophical thought. These conceptions, in turn, dictate the approaches which should be adopted by the interviewer and provide considerations which should influence the client's perception of his own role in the interview situation.

The establishment of these traditions was influenced, no doubt, by the long history which interviewing enjoys. Its use in psychiatric diagnosis, in particular, has been traced to 2600 B.C. in ancient Greece. However, it was only during the third quarter of the nineteenth century in Europe and during the first half of the twentieth century in America that the philosophical foundations of these traditions were clearly formulated within psychotherapy. These traditions still enjoy wide currency within that profession today. Nevertheless, they merit consideration within the compass of this book because they have received some attention from social workers.

Three such traditions are well known and can be briefly described without entering too far into considerations which would normally fall within psychotherapy. There are other less well known traditions but these are rarely applied to the field of social work and do not therefore demand much attention. The three traditions which have received some attention from social workers are the Freudian, the neo-Freudian and the client-centred traditions.

The Freudian tradition, like the others, incorporates philosophical conceptions about the nature of the human personality.

It views the personality as an entity which develops over time and passes through a number of stages, starting from infancy when the child is concerned largely with oral gratification, through to the genital stage. The fully developed personality consists of components which are primordial and unconscious, as well as those which are nearer to the individual's consciousness. The *id* is primordial and has to be repressed, the *ego* and *the super-ego* are, by contrast, subjected to the conscious awareness of the individual. The father of this tradition is Sigmund Freud and his conception of the nature of the human personality as consisting of *id*, *ego* and *super-ego* constitutes one of the mainstreams of Western philosophical thought.

Proponents of the Freudian tradition view the interview as an opportunity for the client to bring unconscious aspects of his personality to the surface and to come to understand their influence as sources of motivation for his behaviour. It consequently places emphasis on free association during the interview, as well as on the developmental processes by which the personality is formed. Free association during the interview requires a relatively passive involvement on the part of the interviewer since his role is largely concerned with motivating the client to communicate and so obtain insight into the deeply-concealed fears which are at the root of his clinical condition. Such insight, it is presumed, would help the client to restructure his own behaviour and thereby alleviate his clinical condition.

This tradition was established in Europe by Charcot and Freud in the later part of the nineteenth century. It took a long time before it was established in the USA. But once it was established, it enjoyed wide popularity and provided a point of departure for the other two traditions.

The second tradition is usually associated with the name of Sullivan. Harry Stack Sullivan started from, and accepted many of the assumptions of, Freud but rejected the passive role which the latter reserved for the interviewer. In contrast to Freud, he viewed the interview as an interpersonal process which actively involves both the interviewer and the client. Both interviewer and client are participant-observers in a process of joint exploration. The interview must therefore provide an opportunity for both participants to work towards realistic and down-to-earth goals. In doing this, the interviewer must pay as much attention to the client's composure, facial expressions, silences and so on as he does to his verbal communication. In actively participating in the interview, the interviewer becomes not only a diagnostic agent in the passive sense in which Freud cast him, but also a therapeutic instrument by which behavioural changes in the client can be brought about. For the client, the interview provides an opportunity to unburden himself by obtaining insight into his self-attitudes and also to work jointly with the therapist towards the establishment of realistic goals. The central implication of this tradition is that the client's clinical condition is the result of his possession of unrealistic goals, goals which are not in any way related to his environment. Sullivan maintained with Freud that insight is important in effecting behavioural changes; nevertheless, he went beyond Freud by his espousal of an active role for both interviewer and client in their explorations towards realistic goals.

Sullivan's ideas were originally propounded within the context of psychiatry and continue to enjoy wide currency within that profession. These ideas are usually described as neo-Freudian because of their relationship to some of Freud's original assumptions.

The third tradition is that associated with the name of Carl Rogers, a psychologist whose main interests lay within vocational guidance. For this reason, it is sometimes referred to as the Rogerian tradition and at other times, as non-directive or client-centred therapy. This tradition is also based on an implicit theory of personality which emphasizes the crucial importance of the self and its need to actualize itself. The self is a product of the human organism and develops out of a continuing process of social interaction in the environment. Since this environment includes other people and their values, the resulting self is bound to incorporate other people's values. The clinical condition of the patient is a result of his distorted perception of such values.

Accordingly, the interviewer's role is concerned with helping the client to restructure his perceptions of himself and of the values which he holds. The interviewer accomplishes this by providing an opportunity for the client to explore his own self-attitudes (a similarity with Sullivan) by not openly directing the latter's actions and not giving advice or criticism. His role is concerned with exploring the feeling-states of the client and completely accepting whatever results from communication with the latter. The clear implication in this is the conception of the client as an individual who is capable of managing his own affairs and who must be made to feel this way during the interview.

These three traditions have received a measure of acceptance from social workers. The Freudian tradition played an important part in the development of social work in the USA, particularly during the early part of this century. The discussions of Mary Richmond were informed by an awareness of the role of developmental history on clients' behaviour. British social work shared this interest in the Freudian tradition, though increasingly, it is being argued that Freudian assumptions should be de-emphasized.

Wootton (1959, pp. 270-3) is one notable writer who has echoed this view. By contrast, the neo-Freudian views of Sullivan attracted little attention outside of the discipline of psychiatry and have not been influential in British social work. Nevertheless, some of its assumptions as to the role of the interviewer have found their way into texts on the skills of interviewing. Similarly, Rogers's assumption that the client's views must remain paramount, irrespective of whether they are positive or negative, has also found its way into interviewing practice. Nevertheless, all three traditions continue to enjoy wide currency within the discipline of psychotherapy. This brief description of their constituent ideas is aimed at illustrating how interviewing can come to reflect the dominant theoretical assumptions of the professions within which it is employed.

3

Cultural factors in interviewing

Our discussion in the previous chapter has shown that the interview situation does not represent a vacuum into which the influence of the wider society does not penetrate. On the contrary, the interview provides opportunities for the participants to bring aspects of the wider society into which they have been socialized—norms, specific values and social orientations—with them. These enter into the interview situation through the social interaction which takes place between the participants. They create *minimum* expectations at the very outset of the interview which, in themselves, derive from the society at large.

Cultural factors, interaction and the interview

There are other more concrete factors which also derive from the wider society and influence the proceedings and outcome of the interview. These are cultural factors such as sex, race, social class, religion, etc. These factors have been widely studied by sociologists, for whom the interview represents as important a technique of research as it is a technique of counselling for the social worker. The influence of these factors is to be seen in the extent to which they create *major* expectations both before and during the interview. They also derive from the wider society and their influence is far more easily recognized in that context than in the context of the interview. Nevertheless, they are as important to the proceedings and outcome of the interview as are the other factors which have been examined in the last chapter.

By referring to them as cultural factors, one indicates that they characterize and set apart specific sections of the community in systematic ways. Social class, for instance, identifies particular sections of the community more or less permanently, thus making identification in society possible. The concept of 'culture' for the

sociologists extends over and beyond this basic element of identification of sections of the community but it represents one of its
most important connotations. To the extent that sections of the
community are identifiable in terms of 'culture', it is possible to
structure social interaction with them accordingly. Cultural factors
therefore relate to a number of characteristics by which particular
sections of the community can be identified.

These factors are concrete because most people are able to recognize them as characteristics which identify particular groups. Social
class is readily recognized by ordinary people, not just as a special
term but also in terms of specific identifying characteristics, e.g.
occupation, style of dress, etc. It is because of this ease of recognition that television, in particular, can depict the social class of an
actor in ways that are immediately meaningful to the majority of
viewers. A brief-case, rolled umbrella, bowler-hat and a dark suit,
all possess relatively clear meanings in the minds of ordinary people
as to the social class and background of a man. Social class, like the
other cultural factors that we shall be examining in this chapter,
constitutes an important component of the consciousness of most
people.

We shall be concerned in this chapter with some of the more
important cultural factors which are important in the society at
large (Alas! we can only discuss a few in the limited space
available) and which could be brought into the interview situation
by the participants. We shall show that these factors influence
the proceedings and the outcome of the interview by creating
major expectations in the minds of the participants. These expectations are described as 'major' partly to set them apart from those
expectations which derive from the influence of the wider society
—norms, specific values and social orientations—which are more
or less independent of the personalities of the participants, and
partly because they provide a more significant source of limitation
on the behaviour of the participants. Their influence in society is
closer to the consciousness of the average layman, but their
intrusion into the interview situation, specifically, nevertheless
remains subtle and unobtrusive. What are some of these factors?
How do they influence social interaction in general and social
interaction in the interview situation in particular?

Social class, interaction and the interview

Social class is one of a number of cultural factors which influence
social interaction in general and which could influence the proceedings and the outcome of the interview.

The concept of social class is one which is widely used in the social sciences because it provides a shorthand way of referring to the combination of characteristics which systematically sets one section of the community apart from the others. It reflects systematic differences concerned with the possession of wealth and education, the enjoyment of different styles of life and the enjoyment of different degrees of influence in society. These differences all turn on the fact that the wider community attributes different degrees of prestige to people according to their possession or non-possession of these characteristics.

Since the nineteenth century, investigators in the social sciences have been concerned to show that much of what happens to the individual in society throughout his life is facilitated, and also restricted, by the social class into which he is born. These differences are not, by any means, confined to British society, but can also be found in other societies. Accordingly, many investigators have argued that while social class stratification may be more important in some countries than in others, the basic separation of people into different sections according to their possession or non-possession of these characteristics is a universal phenomenon. Kingsley Davis (1948, Ch. 14) is one of a number of sociologists with whom this view is associated. We need not concern ourselves with the controversies which have surrounded this view, and which have been touched upon by Cotgrove (1967), Djilas (1957) and Parkin (1971) among others. These controversies aside, however, the systematic differences among sections of the community which the concept of social class aims to capture remain important in British society and exert influences on many aspects of the life of the average individual.

Other writers have argued that the term 'social class' should be abandoned because increasing distribution of wealth and the things that go with it (e.g. home ownership, the possession of durable consumer goods such as cars) as well as the state of near full employment which has characterized Western European societies since the end of the Second World War have eroded, somewhat, the differences which used to set different social classes apart. Yet others argue that social class remains more influential today than it has ever been in spite of the improved economic circumstances which these societies have enjoyed since the end of the Second World War. The finer details of this argument need not concern us here. What remains true, nevertheless, is that no amount of argument about the usefulness of applying the concept of 'social class' to modern British society can deny the fact that there are systematic differences in modern society which the concept of social class directs attention to. It is these differences which remain the foundation for the sociologist's interest in social class as a variable which affects social life.

Many of the studies which have resulted from this interest have consistently shown that social class influences many aspects of the life of individuals. They point to systematic differences between classes as far as affiliation to political parties and the ideas which they represent is concerned. Bonham (1954) showed, in this connection, that the social class of the father is a pretty good indication of the political party which his family would vote for and support in an election.

Other studies show that different social classes have different degrees of susceptibility to a number of diseases. Hollingshead and Redlich (1958), for instance, showed that rates of mental illness differ between the lower class in the USA and the middle class. Even where diseases, as these are commonly understood, are not involved, there are suggestions that medical impairment such as blindness affects different classes in varying ways, according to Hilbourne (1972). Yet other studies show that different classes exhibit differing levels of aspiration about climbing the social ladder, and entertain different levels of aspirations for their children; they also show that social classes differ in child-rearing practices, family sizes, levels of actual achievement in education (given the same opportunities to compete), linguistic codes in their use of the same common language, as well as in personality predispositions. These are only a few of the conclusions which these studies arrived at; they do not exhaust the range of work which has been done on the influence of social class on aspects of social interaction.

However, the orientations, as well as some of the conclusions arrived at in these studies, have not gone unchallenged. They have been challenged on a number of counts. First, they have been criticized because of the inadequate methods employed for measuring social class in some cases. Invariably, occupation, by itself, is taken as the only and, indeed, the most important indicator of social class when, in fact, occupation is only an approximate indicator of social class which should be combined with measures of social prestige, social influence and styles of life.

Second, they have been criticized because they reflect a tendency to use the working class as a useful pool of samples for sociological experimentation. The force of this criticism derives from the implicit injunction against treating human beings as guinea-pigs which Western democratic tradition respects. However, this is not a very crucial criticism because middle class people are also used for the same purpose. Such a criticism is not damaging because it cannot be generalized beyond specific studies and specific circumstances pertaining to these studies.

Third, they have been criticized, most recently by Box and Forde (1971), because the interpretations which are put on data once these have been obtained, reflect a tendency, comparable to a self-fulfilling prophecy, to interpret the low social status of the working class in terms of the same characteristics which are supposed to define them as being of low status. The force of this criticism resides in the implicit charge of 'scientism' (i.e. the deplorable practice of covering well-known and commonplace facts with a veneer of science, in order to gain respectability and acceptance for those facts) as well as in the implicit but false presumption that sociological research resorts to self-fulfilling prophecies.

A fourth criticism is directed at those studies which are concerned with showing that the working class possess one kind of personality, which is different from that found among the middle classes, and which predisposes them to react in specific ways to a number of things, e.g. education and politics (Eysenck, 1954) among others. There are a number of theoretical considerations which are tied up with these criticisms into which we cannot enter in this book.

Nevertheless, these criticisms do not destroy the fact that there are systematic differences among different classes which are important in so many aspects of social interaction in society. Indeed, the significance of the studies mentioned here resides in the fact that they facilitate a deeper understanding of these differences than would otherwise have been possible. It has been suggested by Hyman (1954b) and illustrated to some extent by Hoggart (1957) that there is a common core of value-ideas among the working class which accounts for the high degree of consistency which its members' behaviour exhibits, and which these studies have demonstrated.

It is this common core of value-ideas which provides opportunities for the intrusion of social class into the interview situation, since both client and interviewer could bring different value-ideas with them, according to their social class backgrounds. Since these value-ideas are inculcated into the individual throughout the course of socialization, they would remain an important source of constraint on his behaviour and responses within the interview situation.

Some of the value-ideas which have been investigated concern the tendency among the working class to regard the law enforcement agencies, and other agencies pertaining to their work, as being far removed from their personal lives and as being concerned only with 'doing' things *to*, as distinct from *for*, the working class. Accordingly, they exhibit a tendency to regard not only the police as belonging to 'them' as against 'us', but also the Probation Service or the Child Care Service of local authorities. This is unlike the middle class who perceive a more direct relationship between themselves and the institutions of society towards which they contribute. Hoggart's (1957) illustrations of working class life in Leeds shows how this attitude operates in that context. His observations have been duplicated by studies in other parts of the country and in the USA.

Other differences in the value-ideas of the working class and the middle class have been investigated in some of the studies mentioned here. Some of these studies, such as that of Dohrenwend and Chin-Shong (1967), suggest that the working class possesses different value-ideas concerning how society should respond to deviant behaviour, preferring repressive measures to reformative ones, partly because they are less complicated and more easily understood. Lipset (1963) has attempted, against much criticism, to correlate this attitude towards deviant behaviour with a tendency for the working class to support authoritarian political positions.

Now, few studies have been done on the direct influence of such value-ideas, which are related to social class in the interview and counselling situation. Nevertheless, and their paucity notwithstanding, these studies suggest that the value-ideas of different classes intrude into the interview by creating different sets of expectations, by both interviewer and interviewee, which are not realistically related to the circumstances surrounding the interview. Both sets of participants tend to hold expectations about each others' reactions which are unrealistic. Such expectations would have been nurtured by their social class backgrounds.

One such study by Mayer and Timms (1970) showed that working class clients of social work agencies tend to hold expectations which are at odds with the professional expectations of social workers. Such a clash in expectations reflects partly on the working class clients' lack of understanding of the role of the social worker and partly on the different social class backgrounds from which both participants derive. Similarly, Garfield (1971) showed that treatment following diagnosis in psychotherapy is more likely to be successful in effecting a change in behaviour with middle class clients than with working class clients. Even the tendency to break off casework and counselling sessions in 'mid-course' appears to be related to the social class background of clients, such that working class clients are more likely to do this than middle class clients.

If social class background plays such an important part in the incidence of mental breakdown, in the incidence of blindness according to Hilbourne), in the rate of referral to casework agencies and in dissatisfaction with psychotherapeutic counselling, then the interviews that precede such counselling and treatment situations would have been similarly infused by shared expectations which derive from the social class backgrounds of both sets of participants.

There are other respects in which the social class background of the participants in an interview could intrude into the interview situation. Jordan (1972) and Bott (1971) have shown that different social classes not only possess different patterns of family organization (and many other studies have shown this) but that, more importantly, the consequences of such differences for the management of emotions within the family tend to differ, with the working class tending to see in marriage a more or less convenient arrangement in which 'good' marriage partners do not 'bother each other' unduly. A good husband, according to the value-ideas of the working class, does not 'bother' his wife unduly. Such value-ideas ensure that the management of emotions in the working class family is directed outside the conjugal unit, whereas it is formally directed to the members of that unit among the middle class. Such value-ideas would intrude, undoubtedly, into psychiatric, matrimonial and social casework interviews where the problem under consideration relates to emotional ties within the home.

However, important though social class is in the consciousness of most people, it represents only one of a number of cultural factors which could intrude into the interview situation and of which one needs to be aware.

Education as a factor

Another cultural factor which is just as close to the consciousness of most people as social class, is concerned with the different levels and kinds of education which people enjoy. But in order to examine the way in which education can intrude into the interview situation it is as well to be clear as to what is meant by education in the context of this discussion.

Education can be used to refer to the system of institutions which has grown up over the years and which is concerned with imparting knowledge of a relatively formal kind and in a relatively formal way. Accordingly, the school system in England and Wales has a long history, in which considerations dealing with the kinds of curricula which should be taught have been important, and remain so as social change increases.

The school system, much more than the system of universities, has been known to be tied in closely with social class, since different kinds of schools have always existed in England for the children of different sections of the population. Even where efforts aimed at preventing such differentiation were made, social forces in the

wider society reinforced the association with social class and continue to ensure that different kinds of schools be associated in the
minds of most people with different sections of the population.

Reforms instituted since 1943-4 which were aimed at ameliorating the social consequences of this differentiation have invoked
considerable political furore. The establishment of comprehensive
schools as institutions which would serve a wide cross-section of
the population, irrespective of social class background, has understandably thrown up much controversy, and a number of research-
ers, such as Forde (1968), have shown that these schools have
not, so far, achieved the objectives which were held out for them.

However, there is an intrinsic connection between the products
of the educational system in this formal sense and the range of
people who are likely to present themselves to casework agencies
for assistance. Children with grammar school and public school (in
the English meaning of this term) education are not very likely to
figure among those who seek the aid of social casework agencies,
partly because of their possession of adequate economic resources
and partly because they have alternative sources from which assistance can be obtained. The majority of those who are likely to
seek the assistance of social casework agencies are, therefore, likely
to be drawn from those who are products of the other sectors of
the educational system. In this sense, education as a formal organization for imparting knowledge could play a part in 'determining'
the range of the client population with which the social worker
might be concerned.

Nevertheless, there is another, and more important sense, in
which it can be asserted that education can intrude into the interview situation. This concerns the level of intellectual attainment
which participants bring with them to the interview and which
educational institutions are aimed at developing. Intellectual attainment, taken by itself, can be involved in the interview situation to
the extent that the proceedings in that situation require that interviewer and client handle concepts, verbalize their feelings and their
emotions, and identify non-verbal signs and gestures which are exchanged. This demands facility in the use of all the usual methods
by which communication is usually effected, as well as a somewhat
clear understanding of both the role expectations of the professional
social worker and of those pertaining to the interviewee.

It is tempting to equate intellectual attainment with intelligence
since this is, undoubtedly, a component, but the facility referred to
above includes and goes beyond what is usually referred to as
intelligence. Besides, the concept of intelligence and intelligence
testing in British education have enjoyed a rather unwholesome history, a history which is plagued by controversies concerning the

47

extent to which nature and nurture represent significant components. Nevertheless intelligence, by itself, has never been shown
to play a part in the proceedings and outcome of interviews in any
professional context, whereas there are firm indications that intellectual attainment, whether it takes the form of the degree of
training of the psychiatrist, social worker, or medical practitioner,
or the level of education attained by the client, does tend to
influence the proceedings and outcome of interviews.

Differences in educational attainment of the participants in an
interview can limit or facilitate the exchange of information. Interviews with the 'subnormal' can involve enormous tensions within
the interviewer which could restrict the flow of communication
from his side just as much as from the other participant. Interviewing mental patients, particularly those whose condition is
diagnosed as paranoid schizophrenia, can be most taxing to the
caseworker. This is not necessarily because of their unwillingness
to co-operate with the caseworker but because their condition predisposes them to express themselves in ways which may be difficult
to comprehend. They can be very articulate, but their communication may lack any kind of rational organization of their thoughts.

Nevertheless, the majority of clients who are likely to be referred
to social workers are likely to be relatively normal as far as their
mental health is concerned, even in psychiatric social work. But
such extreme instances clearly highlight some of the difficulties
which could arise in an interview situation as a result of impairment of the mental faculties of participants.

Interviews involving normal persons would, however, reflect the
degree of intellectual attainment which the participants bring with
them to the interview situation because the more educated the
client is, the more likely he is to understand the nature, objectives
and proceedings of the interview, as well as the role obligations
which are attendant upon both interviewers and interviewees.
Mayer and Timms's (1970) analysis of the reasons for clients' dissatisfaction with social casework agencies clearly illustrates this.
Many of the studies described by Garfield (1971) in relation to diagnosis and treatment in psychotherapy also strongly reflect this.

However, it does not follow from this that the relationship between intellectual attainment and facility in the interview situation
is a straightforwardly simple one which can support the presumption that people who are more educated—teachers, university
graduates, scientists, etc.—and who can be assumed to possess a
developed facility for interaction and communication in the interview situation, are necessarily better prospects as interviewees.
Nothing which has been said here justifies this common but extreme
presumption.

48

Smigel's (1958) work with lawyers, supported by the observations of many experienced interviewers, suggests that considerable tension can be generated in interviews with the so-called 'educated' sections of the community, because they are more likely to allow their greater range of knowledge and insight into the proceedings of the interview to impinge on the communication which takes place. Their greater range of knowledge, and past adjustments to interview situations, could actually detract from their concentration on relevant issues. Besides, their more conscious awareness of the objectives and proceedings of the interview can result in information which is 'forced', i.e. is subjected to rational debate in the mind rather than spontaneously divulged. In those circumstances, where the information required by the interview is concerned with opinions and views which are not deeply-rooted in the personality, the responses, and consequently the information obtained, could well prove to be unreliable. This is a problem which is by no means confined to the area of social casework and interviews, but is well-known in the area of psychological testing, in which context it is often referred to as the problem of 'test sophistication'.

The relationship between the level of intellectual attainment of participants in an interview and their responses within that situation must therefore be thought of in general terms. Differences in intellectual attainment would influence these responses to some degree, though the full extent of their influence would vary according to the goal of the interview, the professional context in which the interview is being conducted, and other variable matters such as these. Such differences cannot be used as predictors as to how individual clients would perform in an interview situation. There are other cultural factors which can combine with such differences and influence the proceedings and outcome of an interview.

Race, ethnicity and religion

Race, ethnicity, and religious beliefs are other cultural factors which can, either singly or in combination, intrude into the interview situation and affect the transmission of information. The notions of 'race' and 'ethnicity' are often used interchangeably, especially in situations in which the groups they refer to are in a minority in society. Strictly speaking, however, they should be clearly distinguished, as Gould (1971) emphasized, for while an ethnic group can be represented by a racial minority in a society, racial minorities can consist of various ethnic communities. Accordingly, one might talk of the Negro in the USA as constituting a race, where the underlying intention of the speaker is to establish an implicit contrast with the Caucasian race which constitutes the

49

majority. But it would be a mistake to regard the Caucasian race as consisting of a unitary ethnic group. This tendency for race to consist of diverse ethnic groups is most adequately illustrated in the continent of Africa where diverse ethnic groups, identifiable as tribes, exist under a unitary racial umbrella.

Such a distinction is not as academic as it might at first appear to be, for the social worker in Britain today very quickly realizes that there are significant differences in ethnic values among immigrants who might otherwise be regarded as belonging to the same racial groups. These differences are usually brought into sharp relief in casework situations. Cheetham (1972) has highlighted significant distinctions between various ethnic groups of Indian and Pakistani immigrants in Britain. She has also re-emphasized that there are significant value differences among various groups of West Indian immigrants which the simple use of the notion of race could not possibly be expected to capture. Indeed, one consequence of immigration in the fifties and sixties is that one can talk of black Britons (Field and Haikin, 1971) or black British (Hiro, 1971) without self-contradiction, since the children of early immigrants who have now grown up and been educated in Britain differ from their British compatriots only in terms of skin-colour, not in terms of cultural values or accents.

The differences between ethnic communities can be accentuated where such differences are related to religious values. Some ethnic communities among immigrants possess specific religious values which can be reflected in everyday social interaction. The Sikhs, for instance, subscribe to a set of religious values which influences not only their names but also prescribes their style of dress. The injunction against shaving and cutting of the hair are significant indications not only of their ethnic identity, but also of the religious values which are held to be important. This is, perhaps, an extreme example of the way in which ethnicity and religious values can be closely interrelated. Social casework with Sikhs would therefore reflect both ethnic and religious values.

However, religious values can independently intrude into the casework situation even though their intrusion may not always be as apparent as in the case of the Sikhs. They can influence matrimonial relationships and the authority structure which obtains within families; they can also influence the extent to which certain kinds of medical treatment are considered to be acceptable (as in the objections to blood transfusions among traditional Jehovah's Witnesses). Differences in religious values, as well as differences in ethnicity and race can all intrude into the interview situation in social work.

Their combined intrusion can take a number of forms. First, the communication that goes on in the interview situation may be conducted in terms of the common language of the wider society, but the degree of comprehension which participants bring to their use of this language may differ. This is not a straightforwardly simple matter of the knowledge and use of the English language, but is concerned with the different nuances as well as jargons which participants from different ethnic and racial groups introduce into their use of the common language.

Second, communication in the interview situation is not confined to the mere use and comprehension of verbal sounds but also extends into the area of non-verbal symbols such as gestures and bodily movements. It is common knowledge that different peoples employ different bodily movements and facial expressions. The proverbial Frenchman or Italian not only uses his hands in communication far more often than the average Englishman but the nature of the gestures which he makes are different. Similarly, head and neck movements play a more important part in communication among Indians and Africans than they do among Englishmen. While the exact meaning of a particular bodily movement may not be fully understood in a specific situation, the fact that different ethnic groups and nationalities employ different sets of movements is clearly understood by most people. It is because of this that the English tourist in France or in Italy who cannot speak the local language, justifiably hopes to make his way by using hand gestures. An interview situation which involves participants from different ethnic or racial groups would involve a number of expressive gestures as part of the normal communication which takes place.

Third, the different cultural values to which different ethnic and religious groups subscribe could intrude into the interview situation by creating expectations among the participants which are not 'shared'. Some of these expectations might be based on racial stereotypes and would be unrealistic and false; others may be based on wild over-generalizations. A social caseworker involved in matrimonial counselling with clients from different ethnic and religious backgrounds could well approach the interview situation with conceptions and expectations about the morality of clients which are widely over-exaggerated and are the result of prejudice (in the sense of intellectual prejudgment). But even where this is not the case, such clients might exhibit moral standards about family life, matrimonial relationships and illegitimacy which are genuinely different from those to which the caseworker may have been accustomed. Cross (1969) has shown that strongly held Christian beliefs co-exist with equally strongly held beliefs in magical forces. Jagannhadham (1965) has shown that traditional Hindu ideas impose external pressures on social work in India, which the caseworker must respect. For all these reasons, the ethnic, racial and religious backgrounds from which participants in the interview derive could play a more than superficial part in influencing the proceedings and outcome of interviews.

A number of studies have been undertaken in the USA which are directed towards showing the influence which racial background can have in the interview situation. One of the more notable of these compared the responses of negro soldiers to white and negro interviewers respectively, and is reported in Stouffer (1949). The results of this comparison are best illustrated by means of Table 1.

TABLE I *Comparison of responses of negro soldiers by negro and white interviewers**

Responses	Excess % of this kind of response elicited by negro as compared to white interviewers
Indicating racial protest	21 plus
Indicating low personal commitment	14 plus
Indicating lack of enthusiasm for war	8 plus
Indicating pessimism about post-war conditions	21 plus
Indicating lack of regard for officers and NCOs	2 plus
Indicating low personal satisfaction with the army	8 plus

* Adapted from Stouffer *et al.* (1949).

This shows that the racial background of the interviewer evokes responses which interviewees feel are acceptable. Interviewees dealing with negro interviewers tended to assume that they share the same attitude structure in relation to racial matters. This is what accounts for the observation that responses indicating racial protests and pessimism about post-war conditions in America were evoked more by negro than by white interviewers.

This tendency for responses in the interview to vary according to the racial characteristics of the interviewer is by no means confined to the negroes in the USA. Another study by Robinson and Rohde (1946) showed a similar tendency in relation to Jewish interviewers. The interviewees—all Gentiles—were interviewed and asked to identify the race and religion of four sets of interviewers. One set did not look Jewish and did not introduce themselves by name; another set did not look Jewish but introduced themselves by Jewish-sounding names; the third set looked Jewish but did not introduce themselves and the fourth set looked Jewish and introduced themselves by Jewish-sounding names. The results, summarized and illustrated in Table 2, show a clear tendency for the

TABLE 2   *The effect of perceived ethnic/racial identity of interviewers on responses**

Perceived identity of interviewers	'Do you think there are too many Jews holding government offices and jobs?' (%)
	'YES'
Non-Jewish in appearance	21·2
Non-Jewish appearance but Jewish name	19·5
Jewish in appearance only	15·4
Jewish in appearance and Jewish name	11·7

* Adapted from Robinson and Rohde (1946).

respondents to give anti-semitic responses as their degree of confidence in their perceived identification of the interviewer as non-Jewish increased. By contrast, the proportion is lowest where interviewees felt confident in their identification of the interviewer as being Jewish. The anti-semitic responses reflected in this study were not a product of the interview situation itself but came from the wider society.

Other factors

The cultural factors we have discussed in detail here are some of the most important ones which could intrude into the interview in the context of social work. There are other factors which, though important, cannot be as fully discussed in this book. Sex, for instance, is one such variable which is close to the consciousness of most people and could be reflected in the interview situation as far as the responses that are elicited from interviewees are concerned. There is a tendency for female interviewees to respond differently according to whether interviewers are male or female in relation to certain kinds of questions. An integrated series of studies reported by Hyman (1954, p. 116) showed that female interviewees tend to give more conventional and puritanical responses to male interviewers in relation to certain kinds of questions than to female interviewers.

Other studies, such as that of Mayer and Timms (1970, p. 126) suggest that group affiliation can not only influence the willingness or otherwise of clients to approach casework agencies for assistance, but can also influence the expectations which they hold of the proceedings and outcome of the interview. They showed that working class clients tend to derive some of their expectations about casework from their neighbours, family members, and friends who have experienced casework as part of the total spectrum of expectations with which they approach social casework agencies. This is in line with much of what is known about the influence of group affiliations. Riley and Flowerman (1951) and Festinger (1950), among others, have shown that the extent to which people expose themselves to the mass media and the effect of such exposure on their behaviour are largely determined by their group affiliations.

In sum, the considerations which we have advanced in this chapter show that the influence of the wider society on the behaviour and responses of the participants in an interview is considerable, for not only are the less concrete aspects of social interaction—norms, specific values and social orientations—introduced into the proceedings, but more concrete cultural factors intrude and can significantly influence the proceedings. Undoubtedly, the extent to which any one of the cultural factors which have been discussed would predominate in interviews in social work must depend on variable factors such as the nature of the information required and how deeply-rooted it is. Variable factors such as these make it impossible to generalize. However, they can, in the proper circumstances, impose limitations on the flow of communication as well as on the reactions of participants.

4

Communication, linguistics and the interview

Our discussion in the last chapter was concerned with showing how a range of important cultural factors can intrude into and significantly influence the proceedings and the outcome of the interview. Their intrusion also reflects the important part which the characteristics of the wider society must play in the conduct of the interview. Apart from its technical characteristics as an instrument for collecting information, an interview situation is an expressly human one. It is constituted by human beings with their fads and foibles, their social class, and the educational and ethnic backgrounds into which they have been socialized.

These factors are concretely recognizable by the average layman and form part of the consciousness of himself which he develops throughout the period of his socialization. Their intrusion into any particular interview may not be recognizable, but remain influential nevertheless. The social worker may well be aware of some of the cultural characteristics of his clients and may have obtained such information from various secondary sources before the interview begins. The client, on the other hand, may be equally aware of the background characteristics of the social worker who handles his case. But neither participant would approach the interview situation with anything other than a vague awareness of the possibility that the cultural characteristics which either differentiate or are common to them could possibly play more than a marginal part in the proceedings of the interview.

Yet, it is precisely because the interview is a human situation in which social interaction of sorts must occur, that the cultural factors which we have discussed enter into the proceedings. The consequences of their intrusion can be considerable.

Some qualifications on the role of cultural factors

We have, in the interest of clarity, discussed these cultural factors so far as if they represent extraneous and 'foreign' variables which may or may not affect the proceedings and outcome of the interview. In our effort to be clear, then, we may have left the impression that these variables are not, somehow, intrinsic to the interview situation, but are imported into it. Far from these factors being entirely foreign, they are themselves intrinsic elements which are embodied in the interview situation through the characteristics of the participants, and the social interaction which they engage in. Any interview must therefore bear the marks that pertain to and characterize sections of the population of the society within which it occurs. In effect, then, the cultural factors and the social context of shared expectations which we have discussed earlier are all built into and belong to the interview situation. Wisdom and clarity of presentation, however, demand that they should be treated in isolation from the other more technical aspects of the interview. We shall take up these technical aspects in a later chapter.

But our endeavour to provide a clear exposition may not only have left the impression that cultural factors are somehow far removed from the interview situation, it may also have created the equally incorrect impression that the factors we have examined influence *only* clients, and that the social worker remains unaffected by them, working his way through an interview in a perfect state of pristine isolation from their influence. Our use of data pertaining to client studies (such as that of Garfield, Mayer and Timms) may have reinforced the impression that it is only the client who comes to the interview situation 'drenched' in social and cultural factors. On the contrary, both the interviewer and interviewee come to the interview situation with a range of social and cultural factors. The process of socialization would have left its lasting effects on the social worker just as much as it would have done in relation to the client. For this reason, the social worker, just as much as the client, would reflect the range of cultural factors which we have examined in the interview situation. His social class background, his educational training and his ethnic and racial background would all affect the proceedings of the interview just as much as the background characteristics of the client would affect them. Both the social worker and the client would engage in social interaction using the identification marks provided by these factors.

Similarly, it is often assumed in most client studies that the social worker will be middle class and female and that it is therefore only the social class background and sex of the client which are problematic in an interview situation. This assumption also tends to reinforce the impression that the proceedings and outcome of the social work interview are more significantly influenced by the characteristics of the client than by those of the social worker. This assumption is obviously unreasonable in view of the considerations advanced here.

It is, however, easy to understand how the assumption that the social worker would be middle class and female has occurred. For one thing, the history of social work in both Britain and America includes a range of important personalities who were both middle class and female. One does not require a long list of names to substantiate this point. No list, however constructed, could be complete without mentioning Octavia Hill of the Christian Socialists in Britain, and of the many middle class 'ladies' whom she had to train for social work and who, as Young and Ashton (1956, p. 117) show, irritated her just as much as they pleased her; nor can such a list exclude mention of Louisa Twining and Florence Hill in connection with the care of deprived children or, indeed, Elizabeth Fry in connection with prison reform and the after-care of female ex-prisoners. All these ladies derived from and maintained strong links with the middle class even though some, like Octavia Hill, hit hard times during the course of their lives. Mary Richmond's association with the Philadelphia Charitable Organization Society and the Russell Sage Foundation in America is of equal significance to the development of social work in that part of the world.

A second reason for the assumption that there is a close relationship between being a middle class female and being a social worker is, perhaps, less obvious, and is concerned with the charitable impulse which was so important in the early history of social work in both Britain and the USA. This impulse provided part of the foundation on which the profession of social work was built. It was usually expressed by women before important male politicians, clergymen and missionaries took it up and channelled it into the formation of Charitable Organization societies on both sides of the Atlantic. It is therefore understandable that this impulse was usually expressed in religious and moral tones. The Charity Organization societies which incorporated it accordingly expressed it in religious and moral terms throughout the nineteenth century. This rhetoric employed Christian ideas in the service of helping the 'poor' and 'underprivileged' in the nineteenth century and was comparable to that employed by middle class ladies of the eighteenth century who went 'slumming' to the East End of London.

A third and more contemporary reason for the assumption of a close relationship between being female and middle class is to be seen in the popular image of social workers until recently. The majority of social workers that the average layman comes in contact with have always been women. The majority of social workers today are still women, though they are not necessarily middle class. Klein (1968, p. 203) argues that a significant component in the growth of social work as a profession in the USA was the economic emancipation of women, an emancipation which was in itself helped by the large numbers of women in the USA who always looked on social work as their prerogative. Even today, a larger number of women than men enter the profession of social work.

Nevertheless, there is no intrinsic connection between being middle class and female on the one hand, and being a social worker on the other. Large numbers of males from different social class backgrounds have always been involved in social work, especially medical social work, and clients have always encompassed a wide range of the social spectrum. Increasing numbers of men are now involved in social work—a trend which is bound to continue.

In view of this, Bessell (1972, p. 9) insists that the social worker be justifiably referred to as 'he' in contrast to the practice of referring to the worker as 'she' by most authors. Our use of 'he' in this work is, however, not to be accounted for by the lofty desire of reflecting the contemporary sex composition of social workers today, but by the practical one of ease in writing. The assumption, then, that social workers are middle class and female which is implicit in most client studies is no more reasonable than the impression that the cultural factors which we have discussed influence the interview *only* through the participation of *clients*. The social worker would be as affected by cultural factors such as social class, ethnicity/race and sex as would be the client. Both sets of participants in the interview situation would engage themselves in human social interaction and would, to this extent, be expected to reflect the background characteristics which they bring with them to that situation. It is to the human use of communication by language, both inside and outside the interview situation, that we shall now turn our attention.

Language as a means of communication

The use of language is an important means by which information can be communicated within the interview situation. It is not the only means, since communication by gestures and facial expression is also important. We are concerned here with examining the nature and role of communication in general, to the extent that it impinges on the interview. We are also concerned to show that the linguistic characteristics of a language can impose constraints on communication in the interview situation as well as enhance it. In doing this, we shall show that even if verbal communication exhausted the full range of communication which is possible in the interview, nevertheless different individuals bring different linguistic faculties with them. In addition, the different linguistic characteristics of different languages could further intrude into the extent to which communication between participants is facilitated or restricted. Our discussion in this chapter, then, will show that human communication within the interview situation, though obviously sharing similarities with communication outside that restricted context, is nevertheless as problematic for the proceedings and outcome of the interview as are the cultural factors which we discussed in the previous chapter.

The nature and significance of communication

Many attempts have been made to define communication in a way which would reflect the diverse uses to which it is put, as well as the many forms which it takes in contemporary industrial society. However, it does not require any special powers of comprehension to recognize that these attempts must fail, not necessarily because definitions cannot as a rule, be as precise as one would like them to be, but because the opportunities for communication in social life are so numerous, and the forms which such communication take are so diverse, that no definition could possibly exhaust all the sources of variation which pertain to communication.

Nevertheless, we can approach a working definition of communication by regarding it as the transfer of impulses from one source to another, irrespective of the form in which such a transfer is effected. If we conceive of communication in this way, its widespread application in society becomes immediately apparent, while the complexities which result from its wide application are brought into sharp relief. Television, radio, hints, books, sighs, gestures, etc., are all different forms which the transfer of impulses can take and by which communication can be effected. The use of language is often taken for granted by the average man. But a language, in this sense, is not simply a systematic arrangement of verbs, nouns, etc; rather, the grammatical characteristics of a language take their significance from the fact that communication is effected by the use of that language. Different languages do, of course, possess different grammatical structures. Nevertheless, these differences become significant only to the extent that they facilitate communication by the use of language. It can be asserted, in this connection, therefore, that the distinctive characteristics of a language are to be found less in the analytical elements which constitute it, and more in the extent to which these elements enhance the transfer of impulses and messages from one source to another. This is as true of language as it is of the various other forms which communication can take. Therefore, a gesture of the hands or a kiss between lovers can be as expressive as a language in the message which it is used to communicate.

The nature of the information which is communicated varies with the form which the transfer of impulses takes, so that it can be asserted that *form* constraints *content*. The widespread use and pervasiveness of communication in society, stressed by so many writers (Duncan 1967), does not, therefore, mean the complete absence of any systematic relationship between the nature of the message transmitted and the form which is used to effect such transmission. The relationship between the form and the content of communication is such that a facial expression can indicate only a limited range of information and is restricted to situations in which face-to-face contact is possible. Similarly, a kiss between lovers can indicate a limited range of information concerning the feeling-states of the individuals but cannot be used for transmission of information outside of that range. Similarly, communication by the mass media is largely confined to information of a general nature; it cannot deal with information of a personal nature. The relationship between form and content therefore provides one important systematic constraint on communication. This constraint makes it meaningful to talk about the appropriateness of certain forms of communication for the transmission of certain kinds of information.

However, the diversity of forms of communication and their pervasiveness in social life should not lead one to assume that communication is confined to human beings. On the contrary, communication exists in the animal world and serves the same purpose of transmitting impulses from one source to another, though a lot less is known about communication in this context than about communication among humans. Etkin's (1963) and Brown's (1959, Ch. 1) discussion of communication among animals shows that communication is as functional in evoking appropriate responses among animals as it is among humans. Nevertheless, our knowledge of the vagaries that impinge on communication among animals is imperfect compared with our knowledge about human communication. This is one reason why Cherry (1957, Ch. 1), perhaps too categorically, asserts that human communication is far more complex than communication among animals. The range of information which should permit such a categorical assertion to be made in relation to animal communication is simply not yet available. Far more attention has been concentrated on human communication for this reason. This precludes any meaningful comparison between communication among animals and communication among humans.

If the relationship between the form of communication and the content of the information which is transmitted is one systematic regularity, another equally important regularity is its operation on different levels. Communication takes place on the lowest level from person to person, at an intermediate level from persons as representatives of groups and, on the highest level, from nations to nations. If the para-psychologists are to be believed, communication even takes place between the mortal world of man and the spiritual world. Notwithstanding the scepticism with which this is held by most people, the operation of communication from the lowest level to the highest reinforces its widespread significance for society. It has, in fact, been suggested that not only does communication operate on different levels but that these levels can approximate to the degree of economic and social development of different societies. It is maintained accordingly, that developing countries sooner or later come to realize that their development efforts should include an expansion of communication away from the lowest, person to person, level in the village, in the direction of mass media communication for the nation. The work of Lipset (1963) has reinforced this view, for he shows that the use of the mass media—newspapers, television and radio—is much higher in the developed countries than it is in the developing countries.

In view of these considerations, it cannot be assumed that the widespread and pervasive nature of communication in society eliminates all regularity. On the contrary, the systematic relationship between form and content of communication and its operation at different levels in society are two important regularities which communication exhibits.

These regularities have always caught the attention of experts in communication research in a number of disciplines ranging from electronic engineering and mathematics on the one hand to psychology and linguistics on the other. The former disciplines have been more concerned with understanding these regularities with a view to exploiting technological resources (such as space technology and rocketry), while the latter have been more concerned to understand the extent to which these regularities enhance or inhibit the transfer of messages. However, we do not need to concern ourselves beyond this point with the approaches to the study of communication which have been employed by these various disciplines. The interested student can be referred to the selections provided by Smith (1966) for detailed discussions pertaining to this.

Social factors in human communication

The most widely employed form of communication is language, though we have stressed that non-verbal forms of communication are equally important in society. Our previous discussion concentrated on the nature and significance of communication in general and sufficiently stressed that communication can take a number of forms, of which language is only one. Closer concentration on language reveals a number of factors which highlight its social character and provide it with an 'elective affinity' for the interview situation.

The first of these is concerned with the framework within which communication occurs. This framework has been called 'a communication situation' by Fearing (1964, p. 40). A communication situation refers to the pattern of forces which impinge on the behaviour of participants in the course of impulse transmission, and which influences the extent to which messages are comprehended and understood. This field of forces can be most usefully illustrated by means of a diagram as in Figure 3. The communica-

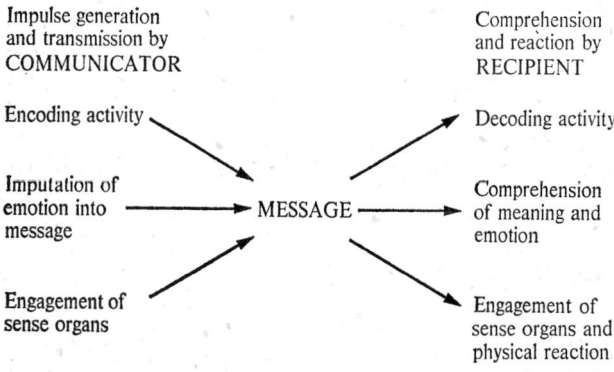

FIGURE 3   *Breakdown of communication flow in a communication situation*

tion situation engages the individual faculties of both the communicator and the recipient in so far as the former must translate the essential ideas that he wishes to put across into a message, using the language which society provides for this purpose, while the latter must de-translate that message once it has been transmitted. In using language for encoding and decoding, both the communicator and the recipient are restricted by social conventions concerning grammatical appropriateness. The extent to which the communicator can get the correct meaning across to the recipient is determined both by his individual faculties with respect to encoding and his facility in the use of the language. The extent to which the recipient can correctly distil the meaning that the communicator wishes to put across is similarly determined by his decoding faculty and his comprehension of the language.

The communication situation is, of course, central to the use of language in society. It is, in itself, not the product of the idiosyncrasies of the individual participants in the communicative act, but is a social product. Similarly, the language which is available for use in communication is equally a social product which endures beyond the existence of individuals.

However, while being social in origin, the communication situation engages the individual faculties of the participants in the direction of facilitating or restricting communication. The encoding and decoding faculties of individuals vary. This is clearly recognized in our everyday description of people's speech patterns as articulate or inarticulate. But even more than this, the differences between individuals as far as encoding and decoding are concerned have been systematically shown to be related to one cultural factor which we discussed in the previous chapter—social class. The facility with which individuals can encode and decode is constrained by common linguistic codes which sections of the population bring to bear on the comprehension of a common language. It is also constrained by their motivation to do so. We shall examine the consequences of such linguistic codes on communication in the interview situation in greater depth later on in this chapter.

What should be stressed at this point is that a communication situation, required by the use of language in society, invokes the social character of a language as well as the encoding and decoding faculties which participants bring to bear on the comprehension of that language. To this extent neither the character of a language nor the coding faculties of those who use it are individual products, any more than a language itself can be described as being an individual product. Though apparently individual in themselves, these faculties can nevertheless be constrained by cultural factors such as social class. Social class can therefore constrain the communication of information in the interview situation not only through the intrusion of those value-ideas which are central to different classes, as we showed in the last chapter, but also in the extent to which it influences the linguistic codes which individuals from different classes must employ in order to communicate. Social influences therefore constrain the communicator's activity, the message transmitted and the activity of the recipient in relation to communication.

A second social factor which is important in relation to the use of language in society is concerned with the meaning which is communicated. Meaning in a language is a shared quality. Language in itself is no more than a set of symbols and their associated sounds which are grouped in systematic ways. The regular groupings of language symbols are permanent and are learned by the individual through the course of socialization. Such groupings and their sound characteristics, as well as the principles by which they are developed, form the mainstream of linguistics and phonetics. These disciplines are therefore mainly concerned with the acquisition of language as a means of communication, and the regularities which characterize languages and permit their use as means of communication. The communicator who uses a language employs a range of commonly accepted symbols in order to arrive at the appropriate compound of meaning that he wishes to put across. In constructing the meaning of the message that he intends to put across, there is a clear but implicit understanding that it will be understood by the other party. Comprehension by the other party is facilitated by the fact that the symbols which are used have definite meanings which will have been learnt. The meaning of the message is thus a product of the socialization process. It is in this sense that language use can be said to involve shared meanings, meanings which are imputed and comprehended by the parties involved in the act of communication.

This element of shared meaning operates in the same way that shared expectations operate in relation to social interaction as discussed earlier. It creates expectations in the minds of both parties to the communicative act as to what a set of verbal symbols will be used to represent at any one time. Indeed, language would simply amount to a set of verbal symbols were it not for the common expectations which both parties unwittingly share in relation to its use. This element of shared meaning is built into the language itself.

However, a lot more is communicated about the expressive states of mind of the parties that can be accounted for by the use of words. Certain tonal combinations in the use of words can indicate the feelings of parties in communication quite independently of any gestures which may be used at the same time. The interpretation of the expressive content of language can be more problematic than the interpretation of the straightforward meaning of word symbols, because the communicator need not necessarily present his feelings in a very clear way. For instance, a speaker who asks politely 'How are you,' can receive by way of a reply, 'I am quite well thank you' with the last two words 'thank you' being strongly emphasized in tone. The interpretation of the feeling state of this respondent in this example is problematic since he could well be trying to state implicitly that 'I'm all right, Jack' or he could be trying to suggest that it is a stupid question since he is not covered up in bandages and plaster. There are, of course, other situations in which the expressive state of mind of the speaker can come through more clearly without, at the same time, being so straightforwardly evident as not to be problematic. For example, a woman could say to her hostess at a party that she is wearing her diamonds, and inquire whether the latter is also wearing hers with the clear intention of humiliating the hostess who may not have a diamond at all. But this interpretation of the feeling of the speaker, though more evident than in the earlier example, is still problematic: the speaker could be asking her hostess a straightforward question about her diamond jewellery, with some prior suspicion that she possesses such jewellery.

Nevertheless, the expressive content of language is as much a shared quality as are the common meanings which words are used to communicate. Languages vary in the scope which they permit for the communication of expressive states of mind, but all languages possess shared expressive meanings as well as common verbal meanings. Both the expressive meanings, as well as the verbal meanings, have to be learnt in society. Society, for this purpose, can be conceived of as a linguistic community which provides opportunities for the young child to, first, babble his way into the fundamental sounds that characterize any language (*phonemes* as they are called in descriptive linguistics) and later to learn the common meanings which are associated with the use of these sounds.

These characteristics—the element of shared meaning and its involvement in a communication situation—point to two common elements of communication in spite of its diversity and pervasiveness. The element of shared meaning is not confined to the parties to a specific communicative act but is general in society as an attribute of language. The same is true of other means of communication such as the use of the morse code; both parties to a communication involving the use of the morse code must possess some understanding of the common meaning which is attached to the constituent dots and dashes, otherwise communication would be impossible. The communication situation is not confined to the parties engaged in the act of communication either, but is general. We can, indeed, conceive of communication in society as being possible because of the myriads of communication situations which are involved, and because of the constant change in the roles of communicator and recipient which goes on all the time. As in the case of the roles of interviewer and interviewee, a communicator at one moment can become a recipient at the next moment.

The roles of communicator and recipient are no more fixed on individuals than are the roles of interviewer and interviewee; they constantly change, and communicators become recipients and vice versa. This is because communication, so central to the interview, is first reciprocal and, second, involves a 'feedback' element (Hartley and Hartley, 1964, pp. 22-5) which allows the person transmitting a message to know whether his message has been received and comprehended. It is because of this reciprocal element and the importance of 'feedback' that it is so easy for a bad interviewer to end up being the interviewee—a state of affairs which would nullify the objective of the interview. There are, to be sure, situations in which this kind of complete role transfer is useful. But in the context of the general run of social work, clear separation between the roles of interviewer and interviewee is usually necessary.

These factors strongly emphasize the social background within which communication occurs, as well as the social nature of language by which such communication is effected. They reflect the fact that communication must perform the function of allowing individuals to adjust themselves to their social and physical environment as well as to relate their position in society to those of other people.

The importance of these functions has been strongly emphasized by studies of children who have been abandoned, or kept in complete social isolation throughout their early life. Such children have been known to lose every recognizable human characteristic, to be incapable of understanding the world around them and to experience mental retardation. On this, the reader can be referred to the work of Davis (1940) and Singh and Zingg (1943). In the case of the so-called 'Wolf Boy of Agra', the abandoned child was reported to have adopted 'animal behaviour patterns' though Ogburn (1959) and Brown (1959, pp. 189-90) suggest that this description may have been the result of over-exaggeration in the reports of informants. This is not to say that communication is the only or, indeed, the most important determinant of how well adjusted the young infant would be in society; there are a number of other factors which are important to the outcome of the socialization process. But these studies do suggest that serious deficiencies, both physical and mental, can arise where individuals lose the social background of a linguistic community.

Linguistics and communication

The development of linguistics as a special discipline concerned with communication by means of language reaches back to the middle of the last century. But the most significant advances were made only after the Second World War, in Europe and America. The areas of interest for the linguistics specialist were once largely concerned with the differences which exist between the syntactical, grammatical and phonological systems of different languages. The specialist in linguistics during the last half of the nineteenth century was accordingly more concerned with trying to understand how various languages in the world differ, than with the problem of how language is acquired and used in everyday communication. Comparative studies of American Indian languages and the English language therefore abound in the early part of this century. These early studies reinforced the impression that language is not merely a means by which people can communicate amongst themselves but is also a store-house of knowledge about the world.

The subsequent development of linguistics moved far beyond such comparative concerns to a number of separate, though obviously, related areas. These areas dealt with the straightforward empirical description of language since it was recognized that any systematic understanding of the nature of language must be based on as complete a description of its basic constituents as possible. Descriptive studies in linguistics have now provided a wide range of information concerning the units of sound which form the basis of any language (e.g. the phoneme and morpheme as units of sound commonly referred to as vowels and consonants) as well as information concerning how children come to learn these basic sounds in their acquisition of language. The grammatical and syntactical foundations of some European languages, such as the English language, are now relatively clearly understood. Accordingly, the discovery that the English language has been changed by its use in America is no surprise to the linguistics specialist, nor is he amazed at the possibility that British and American people can use the same words in the English language even while attributing different meanings to them.

However, interesting though the discoveries of descriptive linguistics may be, they are of little direct concern to the specialist interested in understanding the interview. Language remains an important means by which communication in the interview can be effected, but the characteristics of the language, its syntactical system, etc., are all standard and independent of the participants in the interview. The use of the English language, with its inherent characteristics, is therefore no more problematic for the proceedings and outcome of the interview than is the use of the German language, for example, since it is largely independent of, and prior to, the interview situation. Accordingly, it is of little concern to the social worker, sociologist, or psychiatrist that an interview is conducted by using the English language. The range of information deriving from descriptive linguistics is therefore not directly relevant to the conduct of the interview. Nevertheless, the interested student can be referred to short summaries in Brown (1959, Ch. 1), Brown (1965, Ch. 6), Osgood and Sebeok (1965, Ch. 2), or, in the case of the descriptive characteristics of the English language specifically, Gleason (1965, Chs 2 and 3). The universal regularities of languages are discussed in Greenberg (1966).

What is of more crucial concern to the understanding of the interview is the fact that the language used in the interview situation may constrain, or be constrained by, the thought processes which go on in the minds of the participants. The use of language as the predominant means of communication in the interview can thus influence the proceedings. The problem of the relationship between language and the processes of thinking is one which linguistics experts have discussed increasingly since the end of the Second World War, though experimental data bearing on these discussions has only recently become available, as an increasing number of people attempt to relate the substance of these discussions to various aspects of contemporary life. It is this aspect of linguistics which is of relatively more direct concern to an understanding of the interview, and the role of language in communication in that context.

Therefore, in order to be able to see how language, in combination with the background, personal and cultural characteristics of the participants in the interview, can facilitate the communication of information, or contribute to a breakdown in that communication, it is as well to examine some of the views on the connection between language and thought which have been put out by specialists in linguistics.

Language and thought in linguistics

A number of views have been advanced concerning the nature of the relationship between language and thought processes but we need concern ourselves with only three, since these are more directly pertinent to the processes that accompany communication in the interview situation.

The first of these is usually referred to as the problem of linguistic relativity. It reaches back into the nineteenth century but was clearly formulated by Whorf in the early twentieth century. The hypothesis of linguistic relativity maintains that language incorporates a specific world view unique to the members of the linguistic community which use it; accordingly, speakers of a particular language reflect, by their use of it, a specific approach to the world around them, as if they were all partners to an unspoken contractual agreement to see the world in a common and unified way. Whorf further maintained, as a corollary, that not only do members of the same linguistic community reflect a common conception of the world around them but that language dictates their modes of thinking.

The clear implication of Whorf's ideas is that different languages in the world represent different modes of thinking, modes of thinking which are forever different and relative to each other. In support of these ideas, Whorf adduced evidence drawn from his research into the languages of American Hopi Indians. He stressed that these Indians possess a number of words for the description of a single phenomenon whereas the English language possesses only one. The Eskimo, for instance, possesses three words for the single English word 'snow'. This, to Whorf, suggested that the framework of thought pertaining to snow among Eskimos is different from the framework of thought which characterizes the speaker of the English language.

Many attempts have been made to test these ideas independently and see whether there is, in fact, a systematic relationship between the languages employed by any linguistic community and the modes of thinking which can be said to characterize the members of such a community. Gleason (1961, p. 4) has shown that whereas the English language has a number of words for describing the colour spectrum, the Shona in Rhodesia have only four and the Bassa (a language spoken in Liberia) have only two.

However, it is impossible to work backwards from the range of would very well recognize a number of words such as *powder snow*, conclusion that the thinking processes of the English, Shona and Bassa peoples differ; it is equally illogical to deduce from the range of words available in a language for the description of any phenomenon, the information that the members of that linguistic community are either proficient or deficient in abstract thinking. Anthropologists in the nineteenth century often fell into the illogicality of presuming that where a tribal language provides a number of words for a phenomenon when the English language would use only one, it is because the members of that tribe are deficient in abstract conceptualization. The hypothesis of linguistic relativity is partly responsible for this tendency. But do these attempts prove the validity of the hypothesis?

These attempts have certainly shown that Whorf's observations concerning the possibility that certain languages have a range of words for describing a phenomenon where the English language would require only one obtains in a number of languages. But they do not permit any kind of logical extrapolation from this observation to be made in the direction of thought processes; they provide no justification for the presumption that the use of a number of words in one language where another would use only one indicates anything about the thinking processes of people who speak these languages.

But if these attempts have not proved the hypothesis, neither have they disproved it completely, for proof and disproof are two sides of the same coin. To the extent that they have not disproved it completely, it can be said that discussions about linguistic relativity must leave that hypothesis in a 'stalemate' condition. This state of affairs is to be held against Whorf himself for he failed to realize that the number of words that a tribe, say the Eskimo, uses for describing a phenomenon like snow is a consequence of the importance of the phenomenon in question for its people. Accordingly, Brown (1959, p. 255) has suggested that people for whom snow is important, such as professional skiers and ski-instructors, would very well recognize a number of words such as *powder snow*, *slush* and *crust* where the average person might acknowledge only the single word *snow*.

Second, this 'stalemate' should be attributed to Whorf himself because he failed to realize that the hypothesis of linguistic relativity incorporates a number of sub-hypotheses which should each be tested independently and be found to be valid before anything can be said by way of validating the original hypothesis. For instance, one implicit sub-hypothesis is that language is a determinant of a specific aspect of thought such as perception, or memory, concept-formation and the use of concepts; another sub-hypothesis is that such separate elements of the thinking process can be common among a group of people drawn from the same linguistic community, e.g. one Englishman's perception is similar to another Englishman's perception. Whorf undertook no such differentiation, thus making a proper validation of his hypothesis impossible.

Third, he should also be held responsible for the 'stalemate', because whereas he was prepared to analyse American Indian Hopi language in terms of the number of words they use to describe a particular phenomenon when the English speaker would use only one, he was not prepared to treat European languages in the same way. Accordingly, he did not recognize that his explanation in relation to Hopi language is comparable to the difference between the German saying '*Wie geht's alles?*' (literally meaning, 'How goes everything?') and the Englishman familiarly interpreting this as 'How are you?' Nor would he have been willing to deduce that German and English processes of thought are different. He was merely content to categorize generally the 'average European languages' as being similar to each other in their constituent thought processes. He thus neatly side-stepped the logical consequences of his own illogicality. It is illogical to assume that where a tribe uses three words to describe the 'mouth', it is because they are unable to think of a man as possessing only one mouth. Further, it is inconsistent to make this kind of extrapolation in the case of American Indian languages but not in the case of European languages.

The hypothesis of linguistic relativity therefore remains largely a *hypothesis*, but one whose endurance throughout the development of linguistics since the inter-war years has been such that many people *strongly suspect* that there is some association between language and thought.

A second view concerning the relationship between language and thought is that which is usually associated with a number of psychologists—Vygotsky, Luria, Piaget, Osgood and Bruner to mention only a few. These psychologists all refrain from tackling thought in all its ramifications for they recognize that it consists of a large number of specific motor activities, and that until much more is learnt about the relationship between various activities associated with thought, it would be impossible to do anything more grandiose than to examine specific *aspects* of thought and their relationship to specific aspects of language use.

Accordingly, these psychologists did not concern themselves with thought in the grandiose way in which the Whorfian hypothesis of linguistic relativity tackled it, but concentrated their attention on finding out whether there were connections to be observed between specific aspects of thought and specific aspects of the use of language. Vygotsky (1962) for instance, concentrated on the development of speech in children and its relationship to that aspect of thinking which he called 'verbal thought', i.e. that aspect of thinking which is involved in the use of speech. The young child, according to him, goes through a process in which the relationship between language and thought becomes increasingly inter-penetrating at each stage of his development. One marked characteristic of this development is that the child always masters the syntactical characteristics of speech, without recognizing their significance, and later ties in his use of speech with verbal thought. For him, language and the background characteristics of a linguistic community, provide a strong stimulus to the development of verbal thought in the child, so much so that it can be maintained, without contradiction, that language plays a central, but not the only, part in the development of thought.

Luria's (1957) position is essentially the same as Vygotsky's in so far as he agreed that language development is essentially an aspect of the socialization process without which the subsequent control of behaviour would be impossible. But rather than confine himself to 'verbal thought' as Vygotsky did, he examined the relationship between language and the self-control and regulation of behaviour by the child. As the child masters speech and language, he becomes better able to regulate his own behaviour in relation to others, and develop other aspects of the thought process such as memory and imagination.

These writers all concur with the view that there is a relationship between the development of language in the child and aspects of his thinking processes and that experience with a language impinges on thought and facilitates social learning. Though these writers are clearly oriented towards the implicit problem in the Whorfian hypothesis as to whether language and thought are related, they nevertheless did not approach the problem with the kind of bland disregard of analytical distinctions in their propositions which we have demonstrated in relation to the hypothesis of linguistic relativity; nor did they approach the problem of thought as if the various constituents of the process of thinking are all equally clear to academics; they recognized, on the contrary, that all that could be said initially is that some aspect of the thought processes of individuals appears to be related to their experience with, and the use of, language.

There is, in fact, a range of experimental evidence which seems to bear out the arguments of these psychologists as far as the relationship between language and aspects of thinking is concerned. We cannot enter into an exhaustive discussion of what is fast becoming an expanding area in linguistics, but some idea of the nature of this evidence can be briefly given. Experimental studies of deaf children would be expected to present the problem of the relationship between language and aspects of thought in the starkest possible way because of the obvious limitations to communication in these children.

Many such studies have been done which seem to indicate that deaf children experience deficiencies in their intellectual faculties compared with normal children. For example, a study by Kendall, reported in Ewing (1957) showed that free drawing by deaf children tends to be immature compared with their hearing contemporaries, and that this difference becomes more marked after the age of four years; they were also found to be less socially aware and less capable of dealing with unfamiliar situations. Other studies by Heider and Heider (1940) indicated similarly that deaf children are less imaginative in their play activities compared to normal children. In suggesting that there is some impairment in the social and intellectual functioning of deaf children as a consequence of their obvious difficulty in communication, these studies indicate that while the relationship between language communication and thought may not be as total as the proponents of linguistic relativity would have had us believe, it is nevertheless sufficiently close to call for serious concentration.

Other studies have been done with children with normal hearing which strongly support this. For instance, Shepard and Schaeffer (1956) found that the understanding of the meaning of words was important for children's recognition of objects. In their experiment, only children who already knew what a 'triangle' was, were able to pick out triangular shapes from amongst a range of geometrical shapes. Kurtz and Hovland (1953) also showed that not only is the recognition of objects enhanced by prior knowledge of the meanings of words, but that the memory faculty of children is greater where they know the meaning of words. Their experiment involved two groups of children, the first group of whom were asked to place a circle around words that referred to objects shown to them, while the second were asked to place a circle around pictures of the objects shown to them. One week later, the former group were better able to recognize and remember the objects they had been shown compared to the latter group. These studies with normal children, like those with deaf children, strongly support the views of those psychologists who have been concerned to show that there is a relatively close relationship between the use of language and speech on the one hand and aspects of the thinking processes of individuals on the other.

A third view of the relationship between language and thought is that associated with Bernstein and published in a range of publications. This view recognizes that the thought processes that go on in the mind of the individual are complex and that language itself is somewhat complex in its structure. Bernstein did not therefore direct himself to the gigantic problem of relating language, in all its complexity, to thought in all its complexity; rather, he concentrated more on the various aspects of language use which are related to aspects of the social structure. Considerable evidence is available to show that social structure—social class for one thing—is related to various aspects of education; this evidence has been accumulating since the end of the Second World War but the trend continues unchanged in so far as further research work continues to show that, given the same educational opportunities, working class children do less well in the education system than middle

73

class children. Bernstein took much of this evidence to be correct and sought to show that however close the relationship between language use and thought might be, it is a relationship which is mediated by social structure in general and social class in particular.

Bernstein's argument relates to the existence of different linguistic codes among different social classes and the influence which these linguistic codes have on social learning (1961, 1965), on perception (1958), on hesitation, and on adjustment to the education system. But it is less the applications and more the discovery of different linguistic codes which makes Bernstein's work of crucial importance in understanding communication in general and communication in the interview situation in particular.

He characterizes the linguistic code which applies to the working class as the 'restricted' or 'public' code, and that which applies to the middle class as the 'elaborated' code. The 'restricted' code involves the use of short sentences which are simple in their grammatical construction; statements are broken up by continuous interpolations of meaningless stabilizers such as 'You know?', 'See wha' ah mean?'; the information is put across with the minimum of articulation and with a large number of 'clipped' words, leaving the hearer to draw inferences as to meaning. The 'elaborated' code is characterized by a more complex sentence construction, greater articulation and the absence of 'clipped' phrases or words; meaningless speech stabilizers, such as 'See?', 'You know?', are absent and there is a greater degree of emotional involvement in the substance of the speech, as well as varying degrees of stress to reflect such emotional involvement.

An increasing amount of empirical evidence is now available to show that these linguistic codes do in fact separate working class boys and middle class boys though there are methodological criticisms which have been advanced by Lawton (1970) among others, concerning the measurement of social class, the modifiability of the constituents of speech, etc., which need not concern us directly. Such criticisms notwithstanding, it appears that Bernstein's work 'explains' the now well-known variation between the educational performance of working class and middle class children relatively satisfactorily. His own experimental work (1958, 1960, 1962) has shown that perception and hesitation rates differ between the working and the middle classes. Lawton's (1963, 1970) research study showed that not only are there linguistic codes among the working and the middle classes but that these differences and their constituent grammatical and sentence style are carried over into writing; Bernstein's own work had shown up the differences between the two codes on the basis of the analysis of the speech of his experimental subjects. Lawton's work, however, showed that the influence of these linguistic codes extends into the area of writing and is not restricted to the oral use of language, as Bernstein appears to have supposed (1971, p. 230; 1964, p. 251).

Bernstein's work is justly famous for its demonstration of the existence of different linguistic codes in different social classes who all use the same common language. By demonstrating the existence of these codes, he shows that the characteristics of a language can be separately analysed from the linguistic 'faculties' which individuals bring to its use. It can be justly argued that if different social classes in England apply different linguistic codes to the use of the common language, then comparable differences should be shown in other countries where the English language provides a common medium of communication. Not many studies have been undertaken in other parts of the world where English is widely used. But experimental work by Deutsch (1965) in the USA where English represents the lingua franca shows that children from different social classes utilize language in different ways though he, unlike Bernstein, did not extrapolate from this observation to the question as to whether the different social classes in America must therefore react differently to education. This kind of extrapolation in Bernstein's own work is not logically necessary, though it is understandable in terms of his connections with the educational training of teachers. Lawton (1970), for the same reason, has made this connection between different linguistic codes in different classes, and the problems of educating the working classes *vis-à-vis* the middle classes, more explicit in so far as he calls for intervention programmes in education which would have the effect of ameliorating whatever negative consequences the 'restricted' code of the working classes might have for their educability.

But irrespective of whether the extrapolation is made or not, the three views that we have considered do point to a somewhat close relationship between the use of language and aspects of thought. However, while they suggest a somewhat close relationship, they do not provide any foundation for suspecting that it is language which plays a deterministic influence on thought. Whorf, in the hypothesis of linguistic relativity, comes close to attributing a deterministic influence to language. Fearing (1954), however, has argued that this conclusion is not logically necessary since the relationship could also act in the opposite direction, i.e. from thought to language use. The psychologists are, in general, content to indicate that language and thought are interrelated without entering into the more difficult question as to which directly determines the other, if at all.

Bernstein similarly avoids the question of determinism in his demonstration that there is a connection between language and aspects of thought; he prefers to stress the mediating role of linguistic codes which he identified as the consequence of the intrusion of social class variables, though he has never indicated the core elements of social class that appear to have this effect. These codes might themselves affect adjustment to education but even here, the relationship between these codes and adjustment is not presented as a directly mechanical one.

The conclusion to our consideration of these views must therefore remain guarded; our discussion has shown that there is a relationship of sorts between language and thought and that the two do exert some influence on each other, irrespective, that is, of the mediation of cultural background factors such as social class.

Linguistics, communication and the interview

The three views examined here have been important in linguistics largely because they indicate an increasing concern with the problem of language and thought. This concern can be held to be intrinsic to linguistics as a discipline in its own right. But they have also been important for those who are outside of the field of linguistics because the problem of the relationship between language and thought is crucial to the contemporary world and its social problems. It is therefore no accident that American Indians such as the Hopi, and the Eskimos have featured in early American attempts to test the hypothesis of linguistic relativity; similarly it is no accident that Bernstein's work should have been hailed by educationalists as providing a useful insight into the contemporary problem of the low educational attainments of the working class child compared to his middle class counterpart. The significance which is attached to any scientific work can be said to be directly related to the pressing problems of the day; indeed, some would argue that the only kind of scientific work which is valuable is that kind which attempts to answer and solve some of the contemporary problems which excite people. It is therefore not surprising that extrapolations from Bernstein's work in the direction of educational reform should have been made by people outside the field of linguistics as well as by those who operate within the mainstreams of that discipline.

But there is another way in which the substance of the views discussed here can be looked at, and this is in relation to the problem of communication by language in society in general, and in the context of the interview situation in particular. The demonstration of different linguistic codes in different sections of the community, the demonstration of impairment in the play behaviour of deaf children whose communication is obviously limited by their condition, and the demonstration of a relationship between language use and memory, all have consequences for the ease with which communication can be undertaken within the context of the interview situation. The interview places considerable emphasis on the ability of participants to communicate by language and their ability to comprehend the substance of the communication which is exchanged. Where there are obvious difficulties in communication, as in interviews with mental patients, the blind and children, the amount of information which can be obtained from an interview, as well as the conceptual thinking that is involved in the procurement of such information, must be somewhat restricted. But the impairment of communication among participants in an interview does not necessarily have to be accounted for by blindness, deafness or mental illness. Even where no such obvious difficulties are involved, the linguistic codes which 'normal' participants bring with them to the interview situation could have the effect of restricting communication.

Little is known about the linguistic codes which immigrants possess; nevertheless social work with immigrants often involves problems of communication by language, which are not explained by the relatively straightforward problem of inadequate comprehension of the English language or dialect variations. This could, of course, be a problem which restricts communication, but it is relatively unimportant, since native-born English people could also exhibit the same problem of inadequate comprehension and inarticulateness. What is often more of a problem is that the framework within which emotions are transformed into words, the linguistic codes which are applied to the use of the language, as well as the vocabulary and value-ideas which immigrants apply in the social work situation, are very often problematic. They can be so problematic that a glossary of terms may be necessary even where some immigrants can claim to have been born into the English language. The information communicated in the interview situation can. accordingly, be problematic both for the client as well as for the social worker. The possibility of a breakdown in communication must therefore remain a real one in such circumstances.

This clearly contradicts the widespread but incorrect impression that all that goes on within the interview situation is merely 'conversation'. In a conversation situation, the frames of reference of the people involved are often less problematic than those which are applied in the interview situation. Attempts to 'focus' communication on the immediate object of the interview could well be frustrated by the different frames for verbalization and the different linguistic codes which the participants bring with them into that situation. It is largely because such codes can be problematic that the skilled interviewer comes to interpret and depend on gestural and other non-verbal forms of communication. Non-verbal forms of communication cannot, of course, be seen as alternatives to communication by the use of language except in those special situations where communication by language is obviously impaired; far from being alternatives, gestural and other non-verbal forms of communication go hand in hand with communication by language and are often necessary supplements to the information which is verbalized. The proverbial Frenchman or Italian, or for that matter anyone whose culture predisposes him to gestural articulation, is therefore using his hands as an aid to the mental articulation of words which is a necessary prerequisite for communication by means of language. We shall examine a range of non-verbal forms of communication and indicate their significance for communication in the interview in the next chapter.

5

Non-verbal aspects of the interview

This chapter deals with the non-verbal aspects of the interview which impinge upon the exchange of communication. The previous chapter dealt with the characteristics of verbal communication and the way in which they influence the transmission of information in the interview situation. It showed that communication in society requires a range of common meanings which are independent of individuals but which are common to particular linguistic communities. It also showed that these meanings activate thought processes which are involved in the transmission of verbal communication.

However, communication in the interview is not effected only by the use of verbal symbols; it is also effected by the use of non-verbal forms of communication which possess common and shared meanings that ensure that messages are comprehended by the participants. The use of non-verbal forms of communication is influenced by the personality factors which participants bring with them to the encounter. An understanding of these factors enables the interviewer to chart their operation in the interview situation. It also enables him to understand how the client experiences privacy, how he perceives and interprets the range of his experience, how he construes and internalizes the meanings that he derives from his environment and how he is likely to act in the future. Whatever the immediate goal of the interview, the social interaction which takes place is likely to involve an exchange of perceptions; the operation of all the five senses is likely to be invoked, picking up and exploring cues. Such cues provide the bases on which 'judgments' can be made, and by means of which new attitudes of empathy, acceptance, indifference, tolerance, suspicion, condemnation, rejection and so on can be established. An interview is consequently a situation which involves the fusion of thought, feeling and action in complex ways.

In the face of this complexity, it is not surprising that a number of approaches have been adopted in an endeavour to understand the psychological aspects of the interaction that takes place in an interview situation. These approaches range from the dramaturgical approach which views participants in an encounter as actors playing out roles, through to the empirical approach which uses photography and one-way viewing screens for observing the interaction patterns which result during such encounters. A more recent approach to the study of social encounters involves the use of T-groups and 'encounter' groups by means of which individual investigators are enabled to experience the emotional impact of interaction. All these approaches have drawn attention to the importance of non-verbal mechanisms of communication in particular, and non-verbal aspects of social interaction in general. It is with these mechanisms and with the way they circumscribe interaction in the interview situation that this chapter is concerned.

Signs and communication

In 1916, de Saussure proposed the recognition of a general science of signs which would encompass all the signal systems which are employed by human beings in one connection or another. This science of signs he called 'Semiology'; it includes the signal systems by which communication is effected through language, gestures, musical sounds, symbolic objects and art, among others. According to his view, language can be widely defined as an intricate system of signals of which speech is only a small part; signal systems inherent in gestures, in music, etc., are equally important language forms which are, however, not verbal since they do not require the use of the faculty of speech. They are nevertheless socially based since they involve common and shared meanings. One can accordingly talk of the language of gestures and bodily movements, of the language of music, etc., in this sense.

De Saussure's views did not immediately lead to extensive investigations into the role of signs in communication though it provoked discussion among anthropologists in particular as to the signal elements in myths and customs by which communication is effected. Western psychologists were slow to examine his ideas in the context of communication in small groups. It is true that one can turn to a plethora of laboratory studies on attitude change and persuasive techniques performed over the past fifty years. One can learn, for example, that attitudes are slow to change if faced by horrific warnings and castigations (fear-appeals), that persuasive communications are filtered to recipients via the opinions of their 'reference groups', that although 'credible' communicators are more immediately effective as persuaders, after a time lag, a 'sleeper effect' divorces the message from its source and nullifies the effect of credibility. The question as to whether to place favourable arguments before unfavourable arguments, the virtues of group discussion over formal lecturing, and the effects of multi-group membership on attitude change have all been studied in the experimental setting. The strength of group pressures on the individual has been revealed to be considerable and even sinister; in a study on obedience, Milgram (1963) found that his student subjects were unconcerned about their colleagues to the extent of delivering electric shocks of a lethal nature to them when ordered to do so; other work consistently reveals the absurdities to which an individual will resort in the face of group pressure.

But while the crude facts of social influence have been investigated at length, albeit most often in the artificial context of the laboratory, the minutiae which make up the language of the human signal system have been curiously neglected until recently. Today, an attempt is being made to fill this gap by Michael Argyle (1969) and his co-workers at Oxford, by those in the USA who adopt the 'Here and Now' approach (notably William Schutz and Erving Goffman, among others) and in clinical studies of 'kinesics' ('body language') in relation to symptoms.

Some social psychologists have sought clues for understanding human signal systems in studies of animals in their natural settings. Workers have gone to live with colonies of monkeys and chimpanzees in the field and have brought back interesting findings. Animals communicate with each other by means of a variety of complex non-verbal codes of signs, involving facial expressions, the emission of smells, bodily gestures, ritualistic movements, positionings, and sounds of many kinds. Though there are important differences between humans and animals, nevertheless they both operate from fairly similar biological bases and popular writers, such as Desmond Morris (1967), have seized on some of the new data to back up some premature generalizations.

Some types of animal behaviour (e.g. bird-songs) are learned; fledglings reared away from their own kind cannot produce the typical song of their species. Other types are hereditary and instinctive, such as the patterned language dance of certain bees. Tinbergen and Lorenz have shown how an instinctive sequence such as the complicated mating dance of the stickleback is triggered off by some stimulus in the environment, in this case the red swollen under-belly of the female. Young ducklings develop strong dependency ties on any moving object encountered, whether it is a bird, a human being or even an inanimate object such as a ball. Lorenz called the trigger for such behaviour the 'innate release mechanism'.

It is certainly useful to take non-verbal communication patterns among animals as hypotheses, but direct interpolations such as Ardrey's (1967) assertion that 'the territorial nature of man is genetic and ineradicable' are unwarranted because they ignore the important respects in which humans differ from animals. Studies of animal communication are suggestive; they provide leads to be followed and tested where possible, but our immediate data must be interacting humans in different social contexts.

Nevertheless, studies of animals have drawn attention to the importance of many seemingly unimportant activities such as grooming, teasing and positioning. Such activities constitute a system of signal communication and provide meaningful cues which can be picked up by other animals. Argyle (1969) points to a close parallel between this system of signal communication and that employed by humans. For both animals and humans, non-verbal signals play an important role in regulating interpersonal relationships.

Microscopic bodily changes which accompany aggressive behaviour, sexuality, affiliation, interaction between parents and children, and group behaviour are now being studied among both animals and humans. However, such changes are more difficult to interpret in the context of human society in which people play a multiplicity of roles. The signs and signals of exasperation and aggression which a woman displays to her husband differ considerably from those she shows to her boss, to her work colleagues, to her children, or to an interviewer in a therapeutic situation. Each role provides a variety of constraints and expectations which condition the language she uses. The physiological changes that accompany such signs and language may differ equally from one situation to the next. An understanding of the rich and complicated code of signs by which human communication is effected is crucial for an assessment of how the subject feels during an interview, how he interprets his role in the interview and how he plays other roles outside that situation.

Perception, communication and the interview

Communication, both in the interview situation and outside it, is facilitated by the way people perceive each other. During the 1930s, a change occurred in the explanation of how perception operates in human beings. Before this period, it was assumed that perception took place as a result of the impact of external stimuli on nerve-endings in the eye. These stimuli were then relayed to the brain to produce an atomistic representation of the external object which emitted the stimuli initially—a kind of flat photograph in the brain with each element reproduced faithfully. The Gestalt school subsequently demonstrated that perception is, in fact, a selective process. The brain selects those stimuli that fit certain categories which we already have and provides us with a meaningful pattern or 'Gestalt'; the brain is active in the process of perception and is not merely a passive receptor of stimuli. It is the brain that imposes 'wholeness' on what is perceived. We do not therefore see a collection of bricks, windows and slate when we look at a particular physical object; instead these separate elements are subsumed in the mental category of 'house' which the brain has learned. Accordingly, our perception of a 'house' is molar, not molecular. Human perception is thus molar rather than molecular. It is often noticed that specialists on an interviewing board who have differing frames of reference (as a result of different learning experiences) will perceive candidates in strikingly different ways. They select those cues which fit their individual criteria of relevance, which may reflect a variety of personal needs, interests, prejudices and priorities, as their brains utilize different mental categories for creating 'wholeness'.

Man is a categorizing animal: from his early years, he constructs mental categories deriving, at first, from his infantile and later from his adult, experiences. When he begins to realize that a world exists apart from his own inner experience, that there is a reality outside himself which can be manipulated to a greater or lesser degree, he begins to put parts of his experiences into classes according to certain criteria. He associates certain feelings with certain categories; he feels safe with familiar objects, unsafe with unfamiliar ones. He begins to recognize chairs, tables, motorcars, as well as classes of people. Although there is (usually) only one mother, there may be several sisters, brothers, teachers, postmen, milkmen. Therefore, boundaries of categories have to be explored, accompanied by a fluctuating amalgam of feelings; love, gratification, envy, fury, fear, curiosity and excitement, all come to possess clear but individual emotional meaning. When he perceives the outside world, he tends to select those salient parts which fit his own pattern of experience, his needs and his interests. Jean Piaget (1945) has done interesting experiments with children illustrating the progressive stages of their cognitive and social development. Their categories, and consequently their judgments, become more realistic and less egocentric as biological growth and environmental challenge enable them to develop to a higher level of mental organization. Not only is some order and sense thereby imposed on the 'booming, buzzing confusion' that assails the small child from within and without, but the bases for conceptual thinking and logic are laid.

At first, then, our category systems are pretty crude, rudimentary, and over-generalized, often to the point of absurdity. All smiling men rattling milkbottles are perceived as identical, all black people are supposed to be jolly, older sisters are thought of as being bossy—according to 'our' experience. An over-generalized category which embodies a discrepancy between attributed and actual traits but which nevertheless is held by a number of persons is called a *stereotype*. Certain identifying characteristics are selected as criteria (big nose, red hair, brown skin, etc.). These are then attached to certain other criteria (such as greediness, hot temper, fierceness) which may not be present. The totality is attached to a label such as Jew, Scotsman, Coloured, etc.—and the label conjures up the total image for some individuals more than for others. Roger Brown (1965) believes that a rudimentary stereotyping system in society is necessary because it is impossible to register every single feature which exists in society.

But if the tendency to overgeneralize varies between individuals, the tendency to discriminate among categories also varies equally between individuals. Some individuals can resolve a situation of ambiguity more easily than others. Those who can resolve such situations usually do so by discriminating between categories, while tolerating the stress which ambiguity often involves. Adorno (1950) found, for instance, that authoritarians are more rigid in their modes of thinking and in their categorization than others; Rokeach (1960) describes them as having 'closed' as against 'open' minds in this respect.

The role obligations of an interviewer are such that he must strike an operational balance between overgeneralization and discrimination of categories; he must be capable of perceiving the meaningful patterns which the signal systems adopted by clients project, without, at the same time, concentrating on discriminable features to the point where he loses sight of the 'wholeness' of the client's behaviour patterns. He must equally be capable of recognizing the extent to which behaviour patterns exhibited by clients characterize particular groups of individuals and can, to this extent, be generalized beyond single instances. At the same time, he must avoid the temptation to overgeneralize the true states of feeling of his clients from particular elements of behaviour.

It is not easy to strike this kind of balance, largely because the perception of the interviewer can be 'coloured' by his own conceptions of the sorts of behaviour patterns which different personalities might exhibit. While he may be aware of the dangers of deducing meaningful patterns from discrete elements of behaviour and extrapolating from these to vague overgeneralizations, nevertheless he usually approaches the interview situation with an 'implicit theory' of the personality of the client he meets. He may not be fully conscious of his possession of an 'implicit personality theory' concerning the client he is about to encounter but it can impose a considerable influence on his perceptions of that client. Bruner and Taguiri (1954) have stressed that the 'implicit personality theories' which judges always hold unconsciously, seriously detract from the objectivity which their judgments can be said to possess. Many studies have shown that subjective bias such as may result from the influence of a specific 'implicit personality theory' can seriously detract from the objectivity which one may claim for one's judgments.

In view of this, the interviewer must exercise circumspection in relation to the skill elements which he brings to bear on the inter-action with the client; he must also be circumspect in accepting deductions which appear, at first, to be unshakeable; he must be so fully aware of his own inner world and the extent to which it can deceive him, that he must entertain doubts about both his own perceptions about the client and about the client's actual responses. The implicit personality theories which different individuals hold represents only one source of bias in the mind of the interviewer. What are some of these theories?

Personality models and the interviewer

The interviewer will probably be tuned in to one or more theoretical models of personality when he attempts to penetrate the masks and disguises that he confronts in his client. Some of these masks and disguises will be consciously adopted by the client while others will be unconsciously employed. The interviewer requires a general theoretical framework on which his perceptions of the client can be based if he is not to be swamped by the variety of individuals who present themselves for interview throughout his career. Psychological models of personality are useful for the interviewer in so far as they provide him with a general framework by means of which he can 'categorize' the range of personalities he is likely to encounter and so be better able to understand the kinds of masks which they may present. The interviewer often perceives his client with one or more of these personality models in mind because these models incorporate criteria of relevance which can be used for selecting some elements from the mass of communication which is exchanged in the interview situation.

We can only touch on some of these personality models in this chapter. One such model presents the client as a subtle machine whose behaviour will be predictable once all the relevant facts about him are established. These will include his biological type which affects his characteristic responses to environmental conditioning. There are many variations on this behaviouristic model, and as many techniques of assessment and measurement which can be used in the interview, or as an accompaniment to it. The names of Eysenck (1965) and Skinner (1965) are familiar in relation to this behaviouristic model. Man's behaviour is determined by his conditioning; freedom of choice is illusory; there is no 'ghost in the machine'.

A second model concerns the dimensions of extroversion and introversion. If these dimensions are uppermost in the interviewer's mind, he will be looking for signs of certain types of behaviour during the interview. The extrovert is sociable, he enjoys warm and intimate relations, being more concerned with these than with the task in hand; thus, he would rather be a popular leader than a skilful one. Argyle (1969) notes some elements of non-verbal communication which can be indicators of extroversion, such as eye-contact, proximity and orientation. Extroverts made slightly more eye contact than introverts, and their glances were almost twice as long in the studies reported by Mobbs (1967). Cook (1971) found that extroverts like to sit directly opposite in an encounter; other studies have found that extroverts sit close to the person they interact with.

A third model of man derives from the work of Sigmund Freud and his followers. An interviewer who adopts this scheme will be on the alert for signs concerning the way the client is dealing with unconscious conflicts, the extent to which his ego is in touch with reality, and the extent to which his fantasies and defences are dominant. Freud himself showed how oblique insights could be obtained into unconscious processes and repressed wishes by noting slips, errors and jokes. The way a woman fiddles with her key or wedding ring, how she crosses her legs, the way she shakes her head when stressing the positive qualities of her marriage, her sudden laughter, can all be more revealing than her verbal outbursts. Child psychotherapists provide toys for children to play with and gain much information from the way these are handled. Psychiatric nurses can often tell from microscopic changes in facial and bodily gestures if a sudden change of behaviour in a patient is imminent; clinicians also become increasingly alert to subtle changes in tension which give clues as to where their client is, psychologically speaking.

A fourth model is that presented by Goffman. It views man as being able to refrain from acquiescing in the totality of a role situation by managing his presentation in much the same way that a good actor manages the image he presents on the stage. He does this in order to preserve his personal identity.

A famous description from Goffman (1972) illustrates the possibilities for impression-management which are available to the rider of a merry-go-round in a playground. He describes the child of three or four throwing himself into the role of riding in a serious way, playing it with verve and commitment. He is 'embraced' by the role, in Goffman's terms. The seven-year-old, however, is anxious to demonstrate that riding the horse is not enough; he may try to stand on the horse, or try to change horses without touching the platform. He is saying by his actions, as it were, 'Whatever I am, I'm not just someone who can barely manage to stay on a wooden horse.' He is 'apologizing' for adopting a role which he should have outgrown by actively manipulating his performance. He is not actually denying the role, but the identity of the person implied in the role. By nine or ten, the child feels that the role of merry-go-round horseman is definitely beneath him. He handles the task with bored nonchalant competence, brandishing a candy bar in one hand. A further degree of distance between the role and the true self is achieved by the twelve-year-old who defines the whole undertaking as a lark, a situation for mockery. Maleness for him has become a real responsibility, so he either stays away or jokingly treats his horse as a racing mount, driving his heels into its flanks, and brutally reining it in when the ride is over. Joking is carried further by young adults who display even more distance by crossing their arms, sentimentally holding hands, and guying themselves as performers. Parents who ride with their young children may wear faces that demonstrate that their only concern is for their child; the ride itself is not an event for them. They are stiff and preoccupied with anything but the wooden horse. They can be distinguished from those who project a childish self, meeting the situation half way, but withdrawing from this cast-off self by a little gesture signifying that the joke has gone far enough. Goffman points out that both these types can 'slip the skin the situation would clothe them in'.

This description of role distance on the merry-go-round, which is manifested almost entirely by bodily signs, gives us some idea of the signals to look for in other situations. Each personality model yields signs which can be interpreted by others. When general roles are discussed in the interview, information about how they are played outside that situation, can be gained from facial expression and gestures that accompany verbal communication. The interviewer has to be alert to the degree of involvement and strain his subject feels; he has to be equally interested in how the subject attempts to resolve this strain, in the extent to which he feels an identity apart from that inherent in a role, and in the kinds of fronts or masks which he adopts, either consciously or unconsciously. Finally, non-verbal cues give some indication of the extent to which

87

the subject can 'take on the role of others'; that is, the extent to which he can feel empathy for role players other than himself.

Non-verbal cues: research outlines

We can now look at some of the results of experimental research into particular elements of non-verbal communication even though they are inconclusive and tentative. Argyle and Cook have pioneered this kind of research in Britain but other work has been undertaken in the USA.

Cook (1971) makes a distinction between static and dynamic non-verbal cues. Static cues do not change during an encounter, while dynamic cues do. He presents the following classification of cue units:

Static: face (enduring characteristics)
physique
voice (enduring characteristics)
clothes and other man-made adornments, e.g. spectacles
make-up
hair-style

Dynamic: orientation
distance
posture
gesture
diffuse body movement
facial expression
gaze direction
tone of voice
rate, amount and fluency of speech and meaning

For the rest of our discussion in this chapter, some of these units will be combined in the order in which they may appear to the interviewer in an interview.

Face

The static elements of the face, as distinct from facial expressions, give the interviewer certain basic information as to racial origins, age (within limits) and sex. Certain facial characteristics have given rise to stereotypes with which the interviewer should be familiar. Secord (1959) gave subjects photographs of faces and asked for descriptions of their owners' personalities. The areas of agreement were such as to suggest that there are facial stereotypes; girls with thick lips were deemed to be promiscuous and demanding, negroid types were labelled as happy-go-lucky, superstitious, lazy and dishonest. The face is the area most closely observed during an interview. Children have an innate interest in the human face (Bowlby, 1971) but autistic children and schizophrenics avert their gaze from the human face. This is because the face clearly expresses emotion.

Make-up and hair management are also important elements of face presentation. Men today wear much more hair than a decade ago; their hair is longer, and appears as side-burns, moustaches and beards. Interviewers frequently generalize from hair arrangements, often erroneously. Long haired men, for example, are not necessarily dishonest, unreliable, neurotic or drug-takers. It is dangerous to make pronouncements in this area, as fashions change rapidly over time.

Facial expressions

Facial expressions have been categorized by Eckman, Sorensen and Friesen (1969) as indicating happiness, surprise, sadness, fear, anger, disgust or contempt, and interest. Schlosberg (1954) extends this list to include love, happiness or mirth, surprise, fear or suffering, anger or determination, disgust and contempt. Haggard and Isaacs (1966) noted 'micro-momentary' expressions which change so rapidly that films are necessary to detect them. A classification of thirty-three facial expressions including four eyebrow positions, four eyelid positions, and seven mouth positions was presented by Birdwhistell (1963). He suggests that certain 'kinesic stress markers' such as raising the eyebrows are used to supplement vocal speech.

Body movements

Scheflen (1969) has proposed three dimensions of body language. *Points* are marked by changes in head movements, facial expression or hand movements. *Positions* are phases of an encounter distinguished by changes in posture and stages in a conversation. A psychiatrist, for example, may lean forward when giving interpretations, back when the patient is speaking and providing him with material. A *presentation* is the complete encounter including the bodily movements of entering and leaving the room. Cultural variations obviously affect both facial expression and body movement and should be known to the interviewer. Middle class interviewers may miss many of the nuances of working class clients and vice versa. National differences in body movement should, for the same reason, be learned when relevant. A notation for both facial and bodily points is presented in Argyle (1969).

The hands are as important for expressive communication as is the face. Often hand gestures accompany and reinforce speech. The use of hand gestures varies with cultures. Italians, for example, have a recognized and meaningful set of gestures sometimes given in guide books.

Eckman, Sorensen and Friesen (1969) present five uses for non-verbal cues as a whole. First, they are used as 'emblems' which are put out for deliberate emphasis. Nodding the head to denote agreement, clenching the fist, pointing, all have specific and commonly accepted meanings. Second, they are used to demonstrate that positive attention is being paid to what one is saying. Third, they are used to illustrate what the subject is saying (reinforcing, expanding and punctuating). Fourth, they are used to influence the speaker or demand repetition, a slower pace and so on. Finally, they are used as idiosyncratic signs that are adopted by individuals, and to which they become habituated.

Distance and orientation

Hall (1969) has suggested a continuum of distance ranging from *Intimate* (close), through *Casual* (approximately 5 ft) and *Social Consultative* to *Public* (well spaced). Only intimate positions involve touching, smelling and tasting. There are great age and cultural differences in the amount of touching. Babies are constantly touched and held; indeed, they may suffer damage if they are not touched enough according to Bowlby (1965) and Harlow and Harlow (1962). Jourard (1966) asked students to report on who touched them, and on which part of the body. They were touched on the body most often by their mothers and by friends of the opposite sex—fathers often only touched their hands. In a count of body contacts between couples in cafés, Jourard found 180 contacts per hour in San Juan, Puerto Rico, 110 contacts per hour in Paris, 2 contacts per hour in Gainsville, Florida, and 0 contacts per hour in London. Stroking the body is replaced in adulthood by symbolic gestures such as smiles and nods of recognition which convey affection.

Schopenhauer likened men to freezing porcupines who huddle together to find warmth and are then repelled by each others' spines. This approach/avoidance formulation is developed by Argyle (1969) who accepts that people are both attracted and repelled by each other and resort to an equilibrium position. Pairs of people were placed 2, 6 and 10 feet apart; the nearest one leaned backwards while the furthest leaned forwards to reach their equilibrium point. Proximity increases with liking; it is one way of increasing intimacy, which for Argyle consists of a combination of four variables: proximity, eye-contact, smiling and personal conversation.

Sommer (1969) has studied the ways proximity varies with social setting. People crowd together at a party; they position themselves at approximately five and a half feet for discussions in the work situation. Sommer (1969) and Cook (1971) have noted that people usually place themselves round a table in a way which emphasizes their desire for intimacy in communication. Figure 4 summarizes these positions.

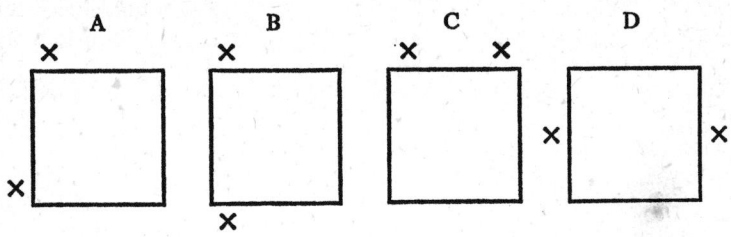

X = sitting positions around table

FIGURE 4   *Sitting positions and proximity in four situations*

A was found to be most common for conversation, B for competition (USA), C for co-operation and D for competition (GB). Research into animals and children shows that a similar distancing process for different activities goes on. Animals have biological mechanisms governing their population density which are instructive; in overcrowded cages they become aggressive; some eat their young and their sexual habits become disturbed. Unlike humans, animals are not normally aggressive in their natural setting. Russell and Russell (1968) relates human aggression to overcrowding and population increase. Hall (1969) compares the use of space ('proxemics') by Germans, English and French. The middle and upper class Englishman who shared his nursery with brothers and sisters and was then sent off to a boarding school, may never have had a room of his own. Consequently he is puzzled by the American's need for a secure place to work in, such as a spacious office. Goffman studied differing settings arranged by people. Some use their office table as a barrier and increase their status by insisting on physical distance and separateness. Others push it to the side and sit alongside to stress equality.

Orientation is closely connected with posture. In his famous hat-rack experiment Mehrabian (1960) asked subjects to talk to a hat-rack which was described as different types of people. He noted differences of orientation and posture. Subjects stood obliquely while talking to those who are presumed to be of lower status and raised their heads when seeking to achieve dominance.

Eye gaze

There are considerable individual differences in direction and continuity of eye gaze. People tend to employ longer gazes when
listening, and shorter ones when speaking. People do not normally
meet eye to eye for more than a few seconds. They look less at
subjects they dislike, and when they are embarrassed or lying. In
some cases a long gaze, especially with wide eyes, may be hostile.
Interaction is often initiated by a period of eye contact, followed
by intermittent glances which provide feed-back.

Argyle reported an experiment in which students were asked
how they enjoyed university life. When given constant eye contact
and reinforcement by the experimenter, they relaxed and spoke
freely. When the experimenter refused eye contact students lapsed
into embarrassed silence. The way a person looks at an interviewer
can tell much about his confidence and integration but it can also
be misleading; salesmen and con-men are practised deceivers in
this area. Considerable work is proceeding on eye gaze by Argyle
and his co-workers at Oxford.

Voice

Non-verbal aspects of speech can be noted when listening to a
tape-recording of a conversation. The timing of speech, its length,
frequency and quantity of utterances, its pauses and smoothness of
synchronisation have all been studied. Chapple (1953) suggests a
standard interview, in which the interviewer systematically inter-
rupts during one phase and leaves long silences in other phases,
while noting the subject's reactions. Bernstein noted that the middle
class use more pauses compared with the working class. Emotion-
ality can be discerned from the character of speech; breathlessness,
trembling, tone and rate are relevant. A vocabulary of the emotional elements in voice production has been attempted by Eldred
and Price (1958). Examples are:

suppressed anger:	high pitch, loud, fast, break-up
overt anger:	high pitch, loud, fast, little break-up
suppressed depression:	low pitch, soft, slow, increased break-up
overt depression:	low pitch, soft, slow, little break-up
anxiety:	increased break-up

Accents in Britain reflect both social class and region; in USA
they are mainly regional. It is possible to identify occupation, age
and physique from the voice, although vocal stereotypes exist
which can mislead.

Speech spectrographs have been used to record and study voice quality. Certain qualities which are peculiar to specific mental illnesses have been identified and variations relating to the progress of the patient have been noted by Ostwald (1965).

Conclusion

In this chapter, we have discussed some of the important aspects of non-verbal communication which can be involved in the interview. Some of the findings of current research discussed are central to the interaction of interviewer and client though they are tentative. The study of body language is important for an understanding of interaction both inside and outside the interview for it enables one to appreciate, among other things, the importance of maintaining areas of privacy, without resorting to the method advocated by W. H. Auden (*Prologue: The Birth of Architecture*):

> Some thirty inches from my nose
> The frontier of my Person goes,
> And all the untilled air between
> Is private *pagus* or demesne.
> Stranger, unless with bedroom eyes
> I beckon you to fraternise,
> Beware of rudely crossing it:
> I have no gun, but I can spit.

6

On interviewing technique

We have so far shown that the interview invokes social and cultural variables that derive from the wider society within which it is employed. We have also shown that it is essentially an instrument for communication and therefore invokes not only the use of language and the linguistic faculties of the participants which the use of language requires, but also a range of non-verbal symbols. This is because the interview situation is an essentially human one in which social interaction must occur. It is, as Bogardus once put it, a social process in which all the characteristics of social interaction in the wider society are brought together and focused within a specific situation. It is because of this that a range of factors that are, apparently, extraneous to the interview situation are nevertheless reflected in it.

However, the technical nature of the interview remains crucial in spite of the extent to which these variables are invoked in its use. The ethical considerations that apply to any profession in which the interview is used must influence the actual techniques which are adopted during an interview. For instance, medical ethics concerning a doctor's reaction to his patients must influence not only the questions that can be asked in a medical interview, but will also influence the way in which these questions are asked. Similarly, a psychotherapist of the client-centred school of Carl Rogers would reflect the basic assumption of this school that the client is capable of understanding his own behavioural short-comings and can, with insight, effect the relevant changes which the therapist wishes to induce. This assumption would influence the kinds of questions as well as the way in which these questions are asked in a psychotherapeutic counselling session. The same is true of interviewing in the context of social work.

Nevertheless, the interview remains a technical instrument which is crucial for the attainment of the objectives of either influencing

94

behaviour or obtaining information. It is in this respect that an awareness of the importance of the operational skills that can be applied to the interview situation is important. The student of social work is likely to be as concerned with the fundamental question of 'how to carry out an interview' as with the various factors which could intrude into the interview once it is set in motion. Indeed, an awareness of the influence of the various factors that we have discussed in the preceding chapters would not be of any significance unless this awareness can be put to use in the actual operational technique which is applied in the course of an interview. It is with this operational technique that we shall be concerned in this chapter.

We shall show that there are certain technical considerations which can be employed in the interview to enhance communication. We shall also show that there are certain psychological considerations which influence the client's response to the interview situation which can be understood by the social worker and put to good use in the interview. We shall be concerned essentially with enumerating some of the technical considerations which must be applied in practical interviewing. The chapter is, in effect, concerned on the one hand with the development of skill in interviewing within the context of social work, and on the other with showing that any interview can be regarded as a collection of psychological forces which both enhance and inhibit communication. It will become clear, at the end of the chapter, that a skilled interviewer is to be distinguished from an unskilled one in terms of the extent to which he enhances (therapeutically) relevant communication.

Technique, skill and method in relation to interviewing

In order to prepare the ground for our subsequent discussion, it is as well to clarify a question which is always pertinent in relation to interviewing. This is the question 'What do you mean by techniques?' This apparently simple and straightforward question is often ignored by writers in social work because the answer it requires appears to be rather obvious and self-evident. Some controversy has revolved around such an apparently simple question. Yet, it is a directly pertinent question since the operational considerations that can be applied to the interview depend on the answers which result from it.

The avoidance of this rather fundamental question has resulted in a tendency for some writers to talk about 'techniques' of interviewing while others talk only of 'the technique' of interviewing. The former leaves the distinct impression that there are a number of different techniques by means of which an interview can be under-taken, whereas the latter leaves the equally distinct impression that there is a uniform set of technical considerations which can be brought to bear on the conduct of an interview. In line with the former, Colcord (1929) discussed the various discrete units of activity that can all be involved in the same interview as 'tech-niques' and thereby isolated some eighty techniques. This approach can have no other effect but to confuse; it is certainly no more enlightening than to isolate separate and discrete elements of surgery and to refer to them as 'techniques' of surgery.

If this approach is illegitimate in the context of surgical practice, it is no less illegitimate in relation to interviewing, for it is the discrete elements which Colcord isolated which, together, go to make an interview; they should therefore be seen as having an intrinsic interrelationship in the interview as a whole.

Some other writers such as Rich (1968) have, more adequately, discussed the operational considerations that pertain to an interview in terms of the professional contexts in which that interview is used. Accordingly, such writers talk of all the operational con-siderations that are together involved in a medical interview, a social casework interview, and a psychiatric interview as 'techniques of interviewing' and correctly infer that the operational considerations that pertain to any one of these interviews would be influenced by the central value ideas which are contained within the parent professional field. It can, in this sense, be asserted that a student of any profession which employs the interview would sooner or later come to learn the 'techniques of interviewing' which pertain to that profession. This is essentially different from isolating discrete units of the series of operational considerations that are employed in any interview and referring to these individually as 'techniques of interviewing'.

The confusion that these different usages of the word 'technique' must have created for generations of social work students could not have been eliminated by reference to dictionary definitions alone because such definitions are formal and devoid of context. Accordingly, the word 'technique' can be defined (as in the Shorter Oxford Dictionary) as a 'manner of artistic execution or perfor-mance in relation to formal or practical details', but such a formal definition could not possibly reflect the different contexts of the use of the word which is evident above. In order to avoid such confusion we have used, as our heading for this chapter, a title which does not imply that there is a multiplicity of techniques by which an interview can be undertaken.

Operational considerations that can be applied to the interview are similar irrespective of the immediate professional context within which the interview is undertaken. It is undoubtedly correct that legal interviewing involves considerations which are particular to the profession of law just as much as social work interviewing involves considerations which are peculiar to the profession of social work. Nevertheless, all interviews are undertaken with the objective of facilitating communication between interviewer and interviewee, irrespective of the professional context in which this might take place. The skills that can facilitate communication in an interview situation are not random but are common to all interviews.

Such common skills are relevant because both the structure of the interview situation and the communication situation (as explained earlier) remain the same in every interview. Every interview involves the two roles of interviewer and interviewee even though these roles change as the interview gets under way. Every interview, irrespective of the professional context within which it occurs, requires that the interviewer and interviewee communicate with each other in relation to the specific objectives which have been clearly specified prior to the encounter. Similarly, every interview involves the psychological dispositions of the participants to varying degrees. The psychiatric interview might invoke such dispositions more than interviews in other professional contexts for understandable reasons. Nevertheless, the psychological dispositions of the participants are usually involved in the encounter in the interview situation. Similarly, communication in all interviews involves the transmission of verbal as well as non-verbal signs. All these basic regularities provide the foundation on which common denominators of skill are based. It is with these common denominators of skill that we shall be concerned in this chapter. It is because these all have the effect of enhancing communication in the interview situation that we have referred to them collectively as 'interviewing technique'.

This does not, however, detract from the point, discussed by Rich (1968) among others, that the professional context in which an interview is employed must influence or determine the choice of skills which can be employed in an interview. Our concern with the common denominators of interviewing skill is based on the recognition that some professional fields might make more use of some of the items of skill that we shall discuss, as compared with others. For example, the importance of building up rapport between client and social worker, which we emphasize later on, can be taken to the extreme of developing a dependant-transference relationship by a psychiatrist. Similarly, an interviewer involved in old-age pensions administration might well dispense with rapport altogether in certain circumstances. But in spite of the varying degrees to which different items of skill are employed by different professions, the common denominators of skill which we discuss remain central to all interviews. To this extent, they all go to form a body of ideas concerning the practical details as to how an interview can be undertaken; together they go to form the 'technique' of interviewing.

Other writers, equally careful to avoid the kind of confusion to which reference was made earlier, have talked not so much of 'technique' in relation to interviewing but more in terms of the 'method' of interviewing. By 'method' they refer to the collection of skills, and the practical considerations that attend their use, which can be employed in the interviewing situation in order to enhance communication. This usage is perfectly agreeable since it stresses that there is a uniform and common body of practical skills which can be employed in interviews, irrespective of the professional context within which an interview takes place. It stresses the point that there are common denominators in interviewing which derive from the basic structure of an interview and from the communication situation which it contains; these common denominators are relevant to the practical execution of an interview, irrespective of the professional context within which it occurs.

Our emphasis on the unity of the method of interviewing has a practical signficance which should be noted. Generations of social workers have been taught by many casework supervisors. The ideas of these supervisors in relation to interviewing become, perhaps naturally, part of the students' conception of the method or technique of interviewing. Elements of the practical experience of these supervisors are taken over by such students and made part of their own interviewing principles and practice. This much is perhaps understandable in terms of the process of education and training. However, such close identification between students and supervisors has the effect of reinforcing the impression that every supervisor has his or her own particular method of interviewing, thus contributing, from another direction, to the tendency to think of interviewing as an operation which involves a multiplicity of techniques. While this is understandable, it nevertheless completely ignores the fact that there is a range of common skills which can be applied to any interview. It ignores the fact that, despite the unique and individual idiosyncrasy which every supervisor would bring to bear on his work with students, there are, nevertheless, common elements of skill which such a supervisor would reflect. The unity of the technique of interviewing is not thereby denied but, on the contrary, is reinforced. Our use of the notion of 'technique' or 'method' is directed towards this common body of skills and their attendant operational considerations. We shall, however, ignore the use of the interview in psychotherapeutic counselling since this would take us too far into the psychological theories and assumptions which pertain to the different schools of psychotherapy.

A related consideration concerns the extent to which it is possible to identify oneself with someone else's style of interviewing and slavishly imitate the technical considerations which such a person may have made his own. It is undoubtedly true that many supervisors of social work students tend to draw on their experiences in carrying out their educational functions. Their experiences in relation to interviewing therefore come to appear as the only or, indeed, the most significant determinant of the practical considerations which the student should bring to bear in interviewing. The student who has closely allied himself to a supervisor's approach to interviewing is therefore likely to be under strong pressure to apply those considerations which have been imparted to him during the course of his training.

However, the practical considerations which are employed in interviewing cannot be slavishly imitated, because the experiences which form part of those considerations vary between supervisors and must, indeed, vary between different interviewers. Further, the situations in which certain components of skill should be given more attention *vis-à-vis* others must also vary. Accordingly, a student of social work who has learnt from his supervisor that complete silence at the beginning of an interview is one way in which a client can be placed at ease might well find that the latter perceives such silence as complete indifference. There are, to be sure, circumstances in which silence can, in fact, contribute towards building rapport between social worker and client. But it would be most unwise to assume that this is always the case, irrespective of the circumstances which attend the encounter between the social worker and the client. To over-emphasize the importance of silence in the interview might well accord with the experiences of a supervisor who is aware that the skilful use of silence remains an important technical consideration in interviewing. Nevertheless, such over-emphasis cannot be generalized over all situations. The student who yields to the temptation to slavishly imitate this over-emphasis on silence might well place himself out on a limb.

The practical considerations pertaining to an interview cannot be slavishly followed irrespective of circumstances. But the core elements which form 'the technique' of interviewing can be learnt. The student who learns such a technique would not thereby become a perfect interviewer by virtue of the diligence with which he accumulated his knowledge. On the contrary, interviewing remains a practical art which cannot be learnt from books but which can be perfected only by actual practice.

The considerations pertaining to skill that we discuss in the following pages must therefore be seen as being fundamental to the practice of interviewing; an awareness of these considerations would therefore stand the student in good stead in the actual practice of undertaking an interview; they constitute necessary considerations which should be borne in mind in relation to practical interviewing; it is, however, only through the actual exercise of interviewing that the art can be perfected.

Our discussion is therefore aimed at demonstrating some of the core elements that pertain to the practical art of interviewing, in all situations in which the interview is employed. Their applicability to particular situations would depend on circumstances which are faced by the individual social worker in the course of his professional duties and the function which the interview is expected to serve in those particular circumstances.

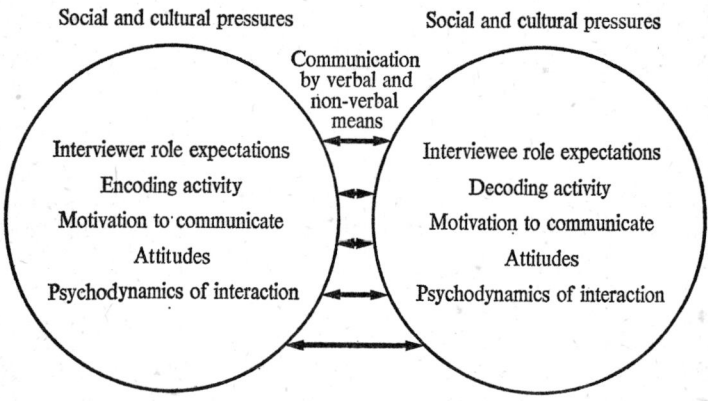

FIGURE 5   *Structural and psychological components of the interview*

Structural and psychological components of the interview

The structural and psychological components that demand practical skill derive from the interaction of the structural features of the interview (described in Ch. 1), and the communication situation (described in Ch. 4) which it contains. We talked earlier of there being an 'elective affinity' between these structural features and the communication situation which is always involved in an interview but in reality the two are even more closely related to each other. In the interest of clarity of presentation, we have discussed the fundamental structural features of the interview separately from the communication situation which is always involved, but these two aspects of the interview are closely interrelated, and together facilitate the use of the interview as a vehicle by which communication can be effected. The interaction of these structural features and the communication situation can be illustrated by means of Figure 5. This illustration highlights a number of components which are central to the interview and which are the central areas in connection with which skill in execution is important. They reflect the fact that the encounter between interviewer and interviewee invokes the psychological characteristics of the participants and 'transforms' them into dynamic processes which, skilfully exploited, can facilitate communication. It is the emergence of these processes which justifies our earlier statement that the interview is a dynamic vehicle, and it is through their emergence that the interview becomes 'more than the sum of its parts'. The skill of the practitioner must at all times be directed towards enhancing communication by concentrating on these components and their attendant psychological processes.

These components and processes can be listed from Figure 5 as (1) the pressure of social and cultural factors, (2) role expectations, (3) encoding/decoding activity in relation to both verbal and non-verbal communication, (4) manipulation of the course of the interview to maintain and increase the motivation of the interviewee to participate, and (5) the psychodynamics of the interaction between interviewer and interviewee. These components and processes involve both participants and are therefore found on both sides of the illustration in Figure 5.

However, some of them make greater demands on the interviewer than on the interviewee. For instance, it can be assumed that the level of motivation of the interviewer to participate in the interview is always high and that, for the same reason, the purpose of the interview is relatively clearer to him than it is to the interviewee. The onus is therefore largely on the interviewer to make the purpose of the interview clear to the interviewee. The extent to which such clarification is available would then influence the level of motivation which the interviewee, in turn, would reflect during the course of the interview.

Similarly, the onus of manipulating the course of the interview so that pertinent areas of the life of the client are explored is also largely on the shoulders of the interviewer if the motivation of the client is to be maintained or increased. It does not, however, follow that the need for communication is necessarily greater for the interviewer than for the interviewee, since the need of the client to 'tell someone about his problems' could have been a very pertinent consideration in setting up the interview in the first place. Indeed, the role of the social worker in our society would be a negative one if all that was required for setting up an interview is the alleged impulsion on his part to (as one writer put it) 'dabble his fingers in the stuff of other men's souls'.

We have referred to these components and processes as being *structural* because they derive from the fundamental structural characteristics of the interview as we described them earlier in the book and are, to this extent, inherent elements in any interview, irrespective of the individual idiosyncrasies which the participants bring with them and irrespective of the professional field within which the interview is employed; we have also referred to them as being *psychological* because the individual personalities of the participants are invoked in the interview in general, and in the processes of encoding and decoding communication in particular; our discussion in Chapter 4 would have shown satisfactorily that even if communication always took a verbal form such as language and even if it is accepted that the use of language is constrained by linguistic codes that come from one's social class background, nevertheless the individual's mental ability and articulateness is always brought to bear on language use. Similarly, the individual personalities of the participants are invoked in relation to motivation within the interview situation, in relation to their understanding of the obligations of their roles as interviewer and interviewee, and in relation to the psychodynamics (i.e. the crises and turning-points) of the interview as a whole. Communication in the interview situation is, in fact, a product of the interaction of all these structural and psychological components which we have outlined.

We can now elaborate on these components and processes. Such an elaboration is necessary in order to show how these components can operate in the *practical* setting of an interview. The range of skills which can be brought to bear on the interview as a whole is usually discussed by many writers on social work in isolation from the various components of the interview to which each one should be directed. The result is often that these skills come to appear as a bundle of practical hints which writers have found useful in their own experiences. This approach would be in order if it can be assumed that students in training are already aware of the structural and psychological components and processes which are involved in the interview. Where such an awareness can justifiably be assumed, discussion of the range of skills can be undertaken in isolation from the background components of the interview to which specific skills should be directed.

However, there is little justification for this assumption. An awareness of the 'theoretical' importance of these components to the interview cannot therefore be taken for granted. The skill factors that should be brought to bear on the practical art of interviewing cannot therefore be treated in isolation from those components of the interview to which they should be directed. So in order to understand these skill factors, it is as well to demonstrate that the components and processes to which they must be directed are not only of theoretical importance to an understanding of the interview but are often operative in the practical setting of an interview.

The impact of social and cultural factors

A client comes into the interview situation with social and cultural factors resulting from the socialization pressures specific to the group to which he belongs, be it a social class grouping or a category of immigrants. His reaction to the interviewer will be influenced by these factors. Increasingly, social workers are having to deal with immigrant clients whose ideas include superstitions concerning witchcraft and magic. An immigrant client who had marital problems with her husband, with whom she had lived for many years and by whom she had had five children, was at a loss to understand how she could be rejected by him. In consultation with the social worker, she emphasized her belief that her difficulties with her husband were caused by the husband's mother, who had originally opposed her marriage and who had been left in the West Indies when the family emigrated to the United Kingdom. In explaining how the mother-in-law's original objections could be sustained through the many years that the couple had spent in England, she expressed a conviction that magical forces were being employed and that these forces are permanent, once invoked, until they are removed by the 'obeah-man'—a familiar technician of magical forces in some sections of West Indian society. She was, in fact, manifesting a cultural belief which characterizes sections of society in the West Indies, even though she had been living in England for many years. Many years of settlement in this country had not succeeded in making her reject the idea that these supernatural forces could explain her marital difficulty, or in making her realize that her problems stemmed from her own domineering tendencies within her own family.

Such a situation is not confined only to West Indian immigrants. Indian and Pakistani immigrants whose children have grown up in this country often reflect the pressure of their cultural background in relation to the amorous connections of their children.

The question of individual choice in the marriage of such children can be fraught with difficulties for the parents who find it difficult to reconcile such choice with family stability and concord. The impact of the cultural background of clients is most obvious in relation to social worker/client relationships where the clients possess a cultural background which involves elements which are very distinct from the way of life of the host society. It is, however, not always confined to such situations.

Certain ways of speaking, such as 'Yes, Love', are specific to different classes in the population as terms of endearment and may well appear to be offensive to the uninitiated ear of the social worker who might expect politeness in social relations as this is usually found but may be put out by such terms of instantaneous but often superficial endearment. An understanding of the significance which should be attached to such terms in given circumstances is important for they more often reflect cultural background factors pertaining to the client rather than elements of communication which should be taken at face value. Such an understanding is crucial to the building of rapport.

Just as the specific values of different cultural groupings can be reflected in social worker/client relationships, so can the social worker's expectation that the norms of polite behaviour will be adhered to in the interview situation. The social worker's expectation that the ordinary forms of salutation and greeting will be adopted, and that the client will not be hostile once the objectives of the interview are clearly explained, is as much of a reflection of his having been socialized into the norms of society as are the specific values which characterize immigrant groups, or other particular sections of the population. If this were not so, the concept of 'rudeness' would not be relevant to social life. For the same reason, care should be exercised in an interview to ensure that conventional forms of salutation are respected, otherwise 'impoliteness' can result, and frustrate attempts at building up rapport.

Skills in relation to social and cultural factors

Three elements of skill which are pertinent in dealing with this component of the interview can be itemized as *purposiveness, emphasis on individuality* and *emphasis on common themes.* Purposiveness demands that the social worker be, at all times, clear about the purpose of the interview. He must clarify this to himself even before the appointment to undertake the interview is arranged. No interview can be expected to reveal its own purpose, otherwise it would devolve into a rambling, aimless, conversation which does not succeed in touching on anything other than the superficial aspects of the client's life. Even if the full implications of the purpose for setting up the interview are only vaguely perceived by the social worker, a clear recognition of the immediate and central purpose of the interview remains important for controlling the process of communication.

One of the serious dangers to be avoided in the practical art of interviewing is that the interviewer can lose his way once the interview has been set in motion. This can easily occur because the dynamics of the interview are such that the communication flow that takes place can be extended in connection with some areas of the life of the client or can be restricted : the communication can itself move forwards and backwards over time and over a number of distinct stages of the client's life. The interviewer, on the other hand, might well find that the client's discussion of some of these areas becomes so arresting that he loses track of the overall picture which should be his main focus of concentration.

The position of the interviewer who is unclear about the purpose of the interview in which he is participating is like that of a third man who tries to deduce the principles that are incorporated in a psychological test such as an IQ test. If he is very good, he might at most deduce that certain elements in the test go systematically with other elements; but he would find it impossible to 'see through' every item in that test. The only person who can do this is the psychologist who either designed the test or operates it and even so, he can only do this if he was himself clear as to the purpose of the test in the first place. Similarly, a survey questionnaire, in the hands of a good sociologist, will include many sophisticated items distributed in such a way that it would be impossible for a third person to 'see through' them to the principles which they incorporate.

However, a proper awareness of the purpose of the interview is not important only because of the need for the social worker to 'find his way' during the actual course of the interview, but also because the interviewer should, at all times, be in a position to control the development of that interview.

An awareness of the central purpose of an interview allows the interviewer to plan, to some extent, the order of procedure which will be adopted. Such a plan must remain somewhat flexible, for while the social worker may be vaguely aware of the sorts of things that must be touched on in the interview if its purpose is to be realized, nevertheless every interview is unique in many respects, unique in the sense that what comes out is often unexpected and spontaneously produced. This is because the interview is not a 'cold' instrument but develops its own momentum and can take both interviewer and interviewee along a number of different paths as it develops. These paths can never be predicted, except very vaguely even by the most experienced interviewer. While planning is therefore essential, the plan which is drawn up must remain so flexible that developments during the course of the interview can be fully taken into account.

A crucial element in any interviewing plan is the division of the interview into a beginning, middle, or main body, and an ending; this division is, of course, not discrete since the beginning of the interview must 'roll' into the middle and on to the ending; similarly, the main body can be affected by a 'bad' beginning; indeed, a bad beginning can make it impossible to undertake an interview by a particular social worker and client, for memories of unpleasant encounters die hard, like memories of supervisors and teachers in the minds of students. This division into beginning, middle and ending is very general and provides a vague and sufficiently flexible framework by means of which the proceedings of an interview can be recorded for subsequent evaluation and analysis.

It is at the beginning of an interview in particular that the impact of the social and cultural factors can be most marked for, at this stage, interviewer and interviewee are without rapport; they had probably never seen each other before; their common resistance to each other may be very high. It is at this point that the need for 'softening up', or, as an American caseworker once put it, 'laying the bait', is most important.

The notion of the social worker 'laying the bait' might appear to be offensive for it implies, somewhat, that the client is 'legitimate loot' to be tackled. However, if one thinks of the social worker as being faced with all the resistance that a salesman has to negotiate to get 'through' to the potential buyer, it becomes less offensive than it might otherwise be. At the beginning of the interview, the client is 'encapsulated' as it were, within his social and cultural groupings; his environment makes sense to him in terms of the categories provided by those groupings; besides, his individual personality is thought of in terms of the way these categories allow him to act 'normally'. The social worker who approaches him is therefore likely to experience the same initial resistance as the salesman who approaches him with a proposition; he may well not be interested in any proposition whatsoever and has to be persuaded, as it were, to become interested.

Where the client is fully aware of the problems which he experiences and may have come to the psychotherapist or caseworker for this reason, the 'softening up' process could be assumed to have commenced; the problems he would have been experiencing would have created an 'opening' which the social worker can utilize. But this may not always be the case. The Probation Officer who has to deal with a youth who has already been sentenced may well find that he has to do more 'softening up' than another who is dealing with youths who have not yet been brought to the courts. The success with which the beginning of the interview is accomplished could then influence the ease with which the main body of the interview itself can be undertaken.

In effect, then, *purposiveness* is not merely a matter of the interviewer being aware of the objective of the interview and, as far as possible, also being aware of the implications of that objective, it also requires that the social worker *plan* the course of the interview beforehand, taking care to recognize that resistance can be high at the beginning of the interview because of the impact of social and cultural factors.

Emphasis on individuality demands that the interviewer must at all times recognize that the experiences of the client are unique to him as a person. His experiences and the attitudes which he exhibits may well fall into a pattern but it could be dangerous to infer such attitudes from prior categories of information. For example, a client may be middle class or working class and it may be known that certain value-ideas are more typically working class than middle class, or vice versa; such categorization may then create expectations in the mind of the interviewer as to how the client will react and the sort of attitudes that he will exhibit. Such information has a role to play in practical interviewing, for it reflects the impact of social and cultural forces on the client's life. But to assume that the experiences which the individual then goes on to relate will necessarilly be typical of the working class is to run the danger of making assumptions about the person from knowledge of the social and cultural category which characterizes him. Most human beings tend to react this way; we tend to utilize a few primary background characteristics and generalize from such characteristics.

This pattern of thinking is often referred to by psychologists as the process of 'closure'. The interviewer is also likely to find himself adopting the process of closure unless he is aware of the danger of premature judgment which it involves; indeed, we often work on this mental element by sticking notices in front of our garages which read 'polite notice' and which then requests drivers not to block our entrances; most drivers would quickly read this as 'police notice' with the greater force of compliance which that usually requires. The client usually reflects the social and cultural pressures to which he has been subjected during the course of socialization, but to deduce aspects of his experiences from this is to run the danger of assuming too much. The needs of the client must be paramount and these can only be regarded as being individual and unique to him. After all, every person is, as Kluckhohn (1948, p. 35) once put it, 'like all other men, like some other men and like no other man' at the same time. Similarly, it could be asserted that similarity of the needs of categories of clients must be expected to turn up from time to time but the person that experiences those needs remains unique.

The emphasis on individuality therefore requires that the interviewer accepts the client's descriptions of his experiences for what they are. He should avoid reading his own thoughts into such descriptions. The fact that a client's mother died while he was under the age of five does not mean that he has experienced parental deprivation since he could have had a mother-substitute (according to the Bowlby thesis) who was quite adequate. Not every slip of the tongue should be regarded as a Freudian slip. Indeed, a client who readily concurs with an interviewer may well be putting on the appearance of responding as he thinks the interviewer feels he should respond—a common danger where the client is very impressed by the authority of the social worker or the prestige of his agency. The client must be assumed, like the proverbial customer, never to be wrong during the course of the interview.

A good guide, in this connection, is for the interviewer to assume that every client possesses an individual social space; this space, if it can be imagined, encapsulates his life and his experiences. The interviewer, at the beginning of the interview, is entering into that space and can meet with all kinds of experiences and resistance which are all equally valid because they occur within that space. In a sense, it is the interviewer who is the 'intruder'; he must expect anything; he must accept everything that occurs within that space as being equally valid during the course of the interview. This emphasis on individuality does not therefore contradict the importance of the social and cultural factors which the client might reflect but reinforces the view that these factors become part of the latter's individual space.

The *emphasis on common cultural themes* recognizes that these social and cultural factors form a first line of defence behind which the true individual is to be found. This is most highly emphasized in social casework with immigrants, but is also true in connection with others. The cultural groupings and their inherent languages, where relevant, provide means by which individuals can be categorized; but they also provide the context within which the true individual can exist; the true self of the person requires these groupings for its existence. The interviewer who is aware of these groupings must therefore work his way through these cultural 'barriers' in order to get to the true self and its social space.

This would appear to be an insuperable barrier where the cultural ideas of the client are far removed from those of the interviewer but as Pauline Young (1935, p. 66) once put it, no two individuals are so *completely* different that there are no common cultural themes which can be utilized as a means of gaining entry into their social spaces. Rapport increases as the common themes of the lives of both interviewer and client are explored. A greeting in Hindustani in New York or Montreal can have a most satisfying effect in a casework interview with an Indian client. Knowledge of West Indian localities or recipes can also have the same effect in casework with West Indian clients. 'Thank you' in Swahili in London can also achieve the effect of creating an opening at the beginning of the interview.

Our earlier discussion of cultural factors in interviewing was not meant to suggest that casework interviewing can only proceed where both interviewer and client either share the same language or belong to the same race or derive from the same social class. This may, in the nature of things, often be the case but is not necessarily so. All that our discussion would have done is to increase the awareness of the potential influence of these factors in general. Such an awareness should make the importance of gaining 'entry' through these cultural factors self-evident. Indeed, the more unfamiliar the setting is in which the interview is taking place, the more salutary would be the effect of common theme exploration in putting the client at ease at the beginning of the interview. The resulting rapport can remain intact throughout the rest of the interview.

However, it must never be assumed that the task of achieving rapport is the same as maintaining it. The ebb and flow of communication in the interview situation is such that rapport, established at the beginning, can subsequently disappear as crisis issues in the life experiences of the client are explored in the main body of the interview. But the achievement of rapport at the beginning of the interview can be aided by the exploration of common themes between interviewer and client. The way in which such exploration is handled would determine whether rapport would subsequently remain intact or disappear as the interview proceeds. Circumspection has to be exercised in the choice of cultural themes to be used for such exploration. This is because certain themes can invoke hostility rather than rapport. For instance, a study of foreign students in the USA revealed what is called a 'sensitive area complex'. Such a sensitivity complex, according to Lambert and Bressler (1954), arises in connection with the role of women, caste ideas and Hindu religion in the case of Indian students in the USA. If it can be assumed that different cultural groups possess similar complexes, then lack of circumspection could lead the interviewer to touch on the cultural themes which bring out these complexes. The result could well be hostility rather than rapport. Circumspection in the choice of themes for common exploration is therefore important. The choice of such themes can only be left to the sensitivity and 'imaginative sympathy', as Heywood (1964, p. 45) once called it, of the interviewer.

Role expectations

Most individuals who are involved in social casework as clients are usually aware of the role expectations which they can hold of the interviewer and of themselves. But this awareness, as Mayer and Timms (1970) showed, is a very vague one. It derives from a variety of factors which are external to the casework relationship. For instance, a married female client who is approached by a social worker might deduce that the latter's role is concerned with her children's welfare. She might deduce that the worker wishes to arrange for the reception of her children into local authority care. Such a deduction of the role expectations of the social worker may be false. Consequently, her own deduction as to what is expected of her would be equally false.

Similarly, a casework agency may have been recommended to a client by a friend or neighbour who would have described the caseworker either in glowing terms (if her own casework experiences were satisfactory) or in negative terms (if those experiences were not). Her expectations as to the role behaviour of the caseworker and of herself would be coloured by such 'secondhand' information. Such expectations may be as false in this case as they were in the other example mentioned above. Such definitions of both the role of the social work interviewer and of the client derive from external factors but are usually operative in social casework.

The development of the welfare state and the range of social casework agencies which that required would have reinforced this tendency among clients to define role expectations, not in genuine, substantive terms but in terms of factors external to the casework relationship. The unmistakable fact is that few clients are aware of the role expectations that should be held of a social worker. The value of the Mayer and Timms study is that it brings this problem into sharp relief. With the increasing scope of training for social workers (and this will increasingly be developed with the trend towards professionalization which was discussed earlier), it can justifiably be assumed that the ignorance of role expectations is all on the client's side.

Consequently, the practical setting of the interview may be

marked by role expectations which highlight the social worker as 'the neighbour's friend' or as someone who 'was real neighbourly' —descriptions which all fail to recognize that while the social worker must, by virtue of his possession of 'imaginative sympathy', be friendly, he nevertheless has a clear job to perform. For this reason, a fund of hostility can often await the social worker's visit, according to the client's original source of definitions of the social worker's role. There is little evidence in client studies to suggest that the full extent of such ignorance of role expectations is fully appreciated by social workers in general. But its existence should demonstrate that practical interviewing involves the social worker in a problematic situation. Such ignorance of the expectations which clients entertain as to his role, provides a gauntlet which the casework interviewer must run.

Skills in relation to role expectations

In view of this, it has been argued by Kahn and Cannell (1957, p. 64) that the function of the interviewer is to teach the client the expectations which he (the client) should entertain both about his own role behaviour and about the role behaviour of the interviewer. Not every social worker would agree with this, since such a teaching function might have the effect of imposing the prestige and authority of the social worker on the client, to the detriment of rapport. Nevertheless, it is a reasonable argument since the interviewer is likely to be much clearer about the purpose of the interview and about the vague outlines of the behaviour that he expects of the client. His own understanding of his role expectations can therefore be assumed to be less problematic, if at all, than that of the client's. He may also have arranged the appointment and may have chosen the setting—the client's home, his work-place or the caseworker's office. He is therefore in a much better position to be alive to the behaviour and processes which might occur in the course of the actual interview. One does not necessarily stand in front of a class to teach, and Kahn and Cannell do not imply that the social worker should undertake formal instruction of the client. The teaching function can be undertaken subtly in social interaction. This, to be sure, is one of the most widely accepted principles of socialization theory. What, then, are the practical skills by which this could be accomplished?

The over-riding consideration here is that the social worker should strike a balance between maintaining too wide a role distance between the client and himself, and becoming too closely involved during the course of the main body of the interview. The danger of maintaining too wide a distance is that the social worker may unconsciously impose the prestige of his position and the authority of his agency on the client in more or less the same way as a policeman's uniform imposes the prestige and authority of his office on a recalcitrant motorist. This would have its effect on the rapport which is established. The client may well feel himself under an obligation to provide 'nice' responses—responses which he thinks are acceptable. The analogy of the policeman's role is quite adequate here. Few recalcitrant motorists, when stopped on the road, would provide anything other than what they feel the policeman should hear, for obvious reasons.

On the other hand, once the interview has been set in motion, the social worker would have to reflect his 'imaginative sympathy' since this facilitates communication without, at the same time, becoming so involved as to blur the line between the client's own experiences and his own. In this sense, 'imaginative sympathy' should be seen as a mental process of identification with a client, in which the social worker puts himself in the shoes of the client without ever forgetting that those shoes are not his, however snugly they might fit. The danger of becoming too involved is not simply that of losing manipulative control over the interview, but also of assimilating the client's experiences into one's own experience. This danger is most serious where a caseworker who is himself experiencing matrimonial problems, for example, interviews a wife or a husband in a similar situation. Only by avoiding direct involvement in the experiences of the client can adequate professional presence be emphasized.

Two of the skills by which such a balance can be struck are *maintaining adequate role distance* and *reflecting social understanding.* The former can be achieved by clear identification of oneself by means of appointments by telephone or by letter. Clear explanation of the worker's objectives in seeking an interview has the effect of stressing role distance as well as indicating professional confidence in one's own role. A policy which indicates that the client can always see the caseworker at any time but which stresses that he must first arrange an appointment also has the effect of maintaining role distance. An interview in the office can also have this effect, provided that the office is not set up so as to appear forbidding to a client. This is one reason why so many social work writers are against the office interview and prefer the home interview. Early social workers like Mary Richmond and Octavia Hill undertook interviewing in the home on the assumption that the client can be encouraged to relax in a setting which is familiar. However, this assumption ignores the fact that an office need not necessarily be austere and forbidding and that home surroundings, while useful in family counselling in which interactions between members of the family are important, are not always suitable for all kinds of interviews.

Social understanding can be reflected by giving the client the appearance of composed (never complete) agreement in communication. This is accomplished by frequent sighs of agreement. The word 'Uh' can be most potent, adequately used, in giving the client the appearance of agreeing with him but never completely falling over into his experiences. It also tells the client that he can proceed with his communication. Such a word is really a nonsense syllable but one which is so commonly used in everyday speech that the client is forced to give it a meaning, in the context of the interview, which suits his temperament at the moment. Another way of reflecting such social understanding is to observe strictly all the usual graces. This involves ensuring that one is polite, that one is willing to postpone the interview to another more convenient time for the client and that one is conscious of the inconvenience which can be caused to a client by the timing of an appointment. This has the effect of increasing the amount of consideration which the client feels is being extended to him. Given a good state of rapport, a client will often decline a properly expressed invitation to terminate, in favour of continuing.

Though these skills contribute towards enabling the social worker to strike a balance between the imposition of too wide a role distance and emotional over-identification, their use must depend on circumstances attending the interview. A Probation Officer who is interviewing a youth who has been to court might find it easier to concentrate on maintaining social understanding in order to ameliorate the authority imputations which have been made on his role by the youth's referral from the courts. Circumspection is required in determining whether to emphasize the matter of maintaining role distance or the matter of reflecting social understanding.

Encoding/decoding activity

Encoding and decoding activities relate to the mental process by which verbal communication takes place. They are concerned with the mental process by which individuals verbalize their feelings by the use of language. These terms derive most evidently from the field of linguistics, as explained in an earlier chapter, but they are always involved in the act of communication within the setting of an interview. The noted studies of Bernstein have shown that the ability of individuals to encode their feeling states and to decode language and so obtain comprehension can take an elaborated form or a restricted form, and that the form which such coding activity takes is related to other social and cultural aspects of the society. Though encoding and decoding activity are most closely involved with the use of language in communication in the interview situation, nevertheless it has been clearly demonstrated in the last chapter that communication within the practical setting of the interview can also take non-verbal forms, i.e. the use of gestures and facial expressions. Such non-verbal forms of communication also require that the client translates his feeling states into a number of bodily movements appropriate to the society within which he operates; they also require that the interviewer be capable of correctly interpreting the meaning which is contained in such non-verbal forms of communication. Some writers correctly refer to such non-verbal forms of communication as 'body-talk'. They serve the purpose of reinforcing verbal communication or alternatively of transmitting messages which cannot be easily verbalized.

Most experienced interviewers recognize that not only do different categories of client reflect differing degrees of articulateness in transmitting their feeling states into language, but they also utilize certain bodily movements more than others. The different degrees of articulateness which are often reflected are due simply to accents; rather variations in accent and dialect probably reflect differing coding abilities in the use of language. This is one implication to be drawn from Bernstein's work. The varying extent to which different clients employ bodily gestures must then be seen as an additional aid to verbal communication. Where speech is impaired, bodily movements take on a greater significance as the dominant means of communication.

There is a tendency among immigrant clients to utilize hand movements in relation to verbal communication more often than native English people. Further, the way in which these movements are executed also tends to be different. Such variations can be reflected in casework interviews in which immigrant clients are involved.

Skill in relation to encoding/decoding activity

Differences in the coding activity of different groups of clients place the burden of comprehension in communication firmly on the shoulders of the caseworker, for he must not only interact with the client in such a way that the latter's inarticulateness does not inhibit verbal communication, but he must also handle his questions and comments so that they will be comprehensible to the client.

The elements of skill which are relevant in this context are the *ability to listen, careful observation, clear question formulation* and *communication control*. The ability to listen is crucial to the execution of the interviewer's role, for he must not only listen to the messages being put across by means of language, he must also be able to distil the additional meanings which inflexions and nuances of speech can convey. The emotional flavouring of the words which are used by the client can often communicate his feeling states and the areas of his life which involve psychological crises of one sort or another. The silences which the client employs can also provide significant clues as to the client's states of feeling in relation to his own problems. This ability to listen to the meaning which is conveyed in speech, as well as in silence, is sometimes referred to as 'creative listening' or 'listening with the third ear' because it requires consideration from the interviewer and an ability to hold back the temptation to interrupt a flow of silence even where the client may be a stammerer or is, alternatively, very ponderous. It is understandable that an interviewer should feel impelled to interrupt and help out a client whose ponderously long silences become uncomfortable. Though such a temptation may be strong, it should nevertheless be resisted, for the thinking process proceeds even during long pauses. Besides, such silent periods can aid evaluation by the interviewer. The social work interviewer who does not say very much in such circumstances can nevertheless be actively involved in evaluation.

Careful observation is demanded of the interviewer because of the important part which facial and bodily gestures play in communication. Such observation can proceed throughout the course of the interview from the very beginning stage, through to the end. Involuntary movements of the muscles of the body can inform the interviewer of the progression of interviewing, since the client is unlikely to be fully conscious of such movements. Indeed, the social worker's skill in observation can be compared here with those of the detective for whom a look of surprise can say more than reams of written confessions. But the social worker's ethical values require that his observations are not the result of trick questions which are directed at invoking bodily movements; nevertheless his observations are as fundamental.

Clarity in question formulation serves to enhance communication by facilitating immediate comprehension and by encouraging the client to proceed with the verbalization of his inner feelings. In this respect, frequent repetition of parts of the sentences of the client can help to show him that he can proceed. Rhetorical questions, though useful in some cases for showing the client that the social worker is familiar with the range of experiences that he is describing, can nevertheless have the effect of destroying the rapport which has already been established. Such questions, like questions with double negatives (e.g. '... not unlike ...?'), should be avoided as they work against clarity. Trick questions are, for the same reason, to be avoided in the social work interview. Leading questions are equally to be avoided.

Communication control demands that the interviewer be fully aware of the directions which communication takes as the interview gets under way. He should be able, subtly and without disrupting the stream of communication flow, to re-direct the concentration of the client to those areas which are pertinent. Only by means of such control can the areas of pertinent information be compressed. Communication control also requires the interviewer to overcome blockages in communication which might reflect the fact that the client has touched on crisis issues. The 'I'm sorry, I cannot go on' response does not necessarily indicate that the client wants to break off the interview, but that he needs help in steering round the psychological obstacle which may have invoked such a response. One way of achieving this is to encourage the client to proceed by claiming full sympathy with his problems. Steering the communication into relevant channels and working round psychological obstacles requires of the interviewer that he understands the psychological basis of the client's reactions.

Manipulation of motivation

Communication control by the interviewer as described above is a form of manipulation of the motivation of the client, since the client is being positively encouraged to concentrate on those aspects of his life experiences which are relevant for the problem under consideration.

Another form of manipulation in order to increase the motivation of the client to communicate can be more pronounced in psychotherapeutic counselling than in the ordinary run of social casework interviews, and can take the form of leading the client not around this time, but into the psychological crises of his life; these crisis issues may have contributed to the problems that he exhibits; they could, in fact, be the 'tip of the iceberg', the superficial indicators of psychological disturbance in the client which he has avoided by building up defence mechanisms. By bringing the client to face these fundamental problems, he can gain insight into himself and come to cope with them more.

The social worker is often advised to avoid creating tension by bringing the client into direct confrontation with himself because of the importance of respecting the integrity of the individual. But in psychotherapeutic counselling, it may sometimes be necessary to work towards a direct, and if necessary, violent confrontation of the psychological issues that form the focus of the client's problems. Such extreme forms of manipulation are often adopted by the psychiatrist in his use of hypnosis. Accordingly, the female client who avoids the difficult recognition that her mother has always been a competitor for the sexual attractions of men may often hide this possibility under the belief that she loves her mother and models herself on her. Similarly, incestuous relationships between fathers and daughters can create unconscious guilt complexes that cannot be faced directly. In such cases, direct confrontation and all the psychological tension which might result from such confrontation should become an immediate goal for the interviewer. Such extreme forms of manipulation are not usually required in the ordinary run of social casework. In the last analysis, every interview can be said to involve a certain amount of mental manipulation in so far as the interviewer seeks to bring about an orientation in the mind of the client which would facilitate communication. But the social work interviewer does not usually take such manipulation to the extremes that are sometimes required in psychotherapy and psychiatry.

The skills employed by the social worker in order to bring about this minimal degree of manipulation often consist of encouragement to the client to communicate and express his problems, of assurances as to the confidentiality of such communication, and of appeals to the vanity of the client by deliberately giving him the impression that he is praiseworthy, as well as convincing him that he is not unique in experiencing the problems under discussion. They also include persuading him to believe that the social worker is fully alive to the difficulties that are under consideration because he has himself experienced them, together with an unhurried appearance in the execution of the interview, in order to leave the client with the impression that the interview is his very own moment.

Psychodynamics of interaction

A range of psychological processes are invoked during the course of the interview, even though neither interviewer nor client might be aware that such processes are in operation. The processes by which rapport is established between the interviewer and the client, the warmth that is exhibited in the encounter, the processes by which crisis points in the life experiences of the client are unearthed, and the ebb and flow of communication, all form part of the psychodynamic element in the interview. No two interviews can ever be alike because the psychological personalities which invoke these processes are always different. Consequently, the impact of an interview on the participants is usually such that significant memory traces are left. There are no studies of the extent to which clients and interviewers are able to recall their experiences during interviews in which they have participated, but the collection of studies reported by Hyman (1954) suggest that most participants can remember the way they felt during the course of interviews in which they took part.

Bogardus (1936) has put forward an interesting theory of how the psychodynamic processes which emerge in the interview work for the development of rapport and motivation. He effectively shows that the beginning, middle and ending of an interview are usually integrated into a whole and cannot be seen as separate elements. Consequently, every interview is seen as a whole and 'survives' as such, or is disrupted and fails. It would therefore be impossible to accomplish the beginning stages of an interview on one occasion and to have the progression to the middle stages disrupted and postponed for another occasion.

The essence of the theory is quite interesting and is expressed in simple psychological terms. It argues that, first, each participant in an interview provides a stimulus to communication in the interview situation which invokes an appropriate response from the other party. The effect of such a response is to create a certain level of knowledge about each other and about the conditions under consideration. This level then becomes another stimulus which invokes a further response and thus establishes a higher level of knowledge about the participants (p. 114).

This can be expressed in the language of field theory to much greater effect since an interview is not merely a collection of stimuli and responses. The learning theory language in which Bogardus originally expressed the theory is useful but runs the risk of presenting an interview as a series of separate and discrete stimulus and response elements. An interview consists of more than stimuli and responses. The impact of Bogardus's theory can be more fully appreciated by expressing it in terms of the language of field theory (Lewin, 1951). Kahn and Cannell (1957, p. 58) come close to doing this in their discussion of the constant change in the psychological field of the respondent.

Each participant in the interview can be seen as possessing a field of psychological forces around him—call it his social space or his life space. An interview involves the conjunction of the life spaces, with their inherent psychological forces, of interviewer and client. The initiation of an encounter between the participants will create a disruption of each field of forces. The progression of the interview will then involve a 'restructuring' of the life spaces of both participants. During the course of the interview, each participant will attempt to 'defend' his life space in order to resist the possibility of disruption. But the termination of a successful interview must see the participants 'back' with their 'restructured' life spaces intact once more.

One need not accept this elaboration of Bogardus's theory; nevertheless it does enable the question to be asked: What happens if the interview is broken off in mid-stream? 'Unstructured' life spaces are distressful to the personality and this distress can have physiological concomitants. Some of the studies discussed by Matarazzo (1965, p. 419), show that the pulse rate of interviewers and interviewees varies concomitantly during the course of interviewing as the life spaces of participants become unstructured. The interested reader can pursue this in Matarazzo's paper.

Nevertheless, these studies as well as Bogardus's theory should sufficiently stress that an interview is more than just a superficial encounter between persons; rather, the interaction of stimuli and responses in the interview results in a *spiral* of understanding and *rapport*. This part of Bogardus's theory is, for this reason, often referred to as the *theory of spiral or circular response*. The second part of his theory relates to the way in which the accumulation of stimuli and responses affects the progression of the interview, and maintains that the interaction of stimuli and responses in the interview and the progression to higher levels of knowledge means that initial steps in an interview strongly determine the subsequent progression of the interview: 'An initial stimulus may be followed by either an agreeable or by a disagreeable response, and a cumulative process of agreeableness and of rapport is set in motion, or a cumulative process of disagreeableness and antagonism obtains momentum.' (p. 117). Accordingly, this part of Bogardus's theory is usually referred to as the *theory of cumulative response*. But both parts strongly stress that the psychodynamic processes that are invoked in the interview are closely interrelated and are significant for the outcome.

The various skill factors which we have discussed, as well as the attitudes which they require on the part of the interviewer, are all therefore interrelated in the interview since they contribute to the extent to which these psychodynamic processes can be set in motion and a successful interview achieved for both interviewer and client. They are much more than simply hints on the practical art of interviewing, for their importance reflects the wholeness of the interviewing procedure in general.

7

Traditions of interviewing: practical considerations

The previous chapter dealt with the technical and practical skills which the interviewer adopts during the course of interviewing and counselling in order to facilitate communication with the client and, through this, to influence his attitudes and behaviour. These skills are all directed to the various components of the structure of the interview and together constitute the technique by which an interview can be undertaken. However, the application of these skills does not take place in a vacuum for, as we have demonstrated earlier, the value assumptions of the professional context within which the interview is employed can influence the theoretical considerations which the interviewer brings to bear on his practical activities. These considerations have, over time, been incorporated in a number of therapy systems, schools of thought or traditions of interviewing in psychotherapy in particular. The Freudian, Sullivanian and Rogerian schools of thought were briefly illustrated in Chapter 2.

In this chapter, we shall examine some of the practical issues which are involved in the application of these schools of thought in the interviewing situation. We shall show that these issues are as relevant to the activities of the social worker as they are to the activities of the psychotherapist. For the purpose of this examination and in the light of the discussion in Chapter 1, we shall use the terms 'interviewing' and 'counselling' interchangeably, partly because the traditions of interviewing developed largely within psychotherapy and partly because therapeutic situations provide the best illustrations of how these traditions can influence the process of interviewing, and are often involved in social work.

The social worker as a therapist

With very few exceptions, the social work interview is basically therapeutic in nature. The longer the period of social interaction between counsellor and client, the more therapeutic it becomes. It is important, therefore, that the traditions and phases of a therapeutic interaction such as is involved in the interview are fully understood. Social interaction is defined as two or more people interacting, and therapy is defined as that which is provided by a therapist with the aim of changing the overt and covert behaviour of his client. Therapeutic interaction may therefore be defined as two or more people interacting in a social situation with the aim of bringing about desirable changes in the one with the aid of the other.

It may well be said that social workers are not therapists, but in reality anyone involved in helping others to manage their problems is a therapist. A psychiatrist, psychologist, social worker, probation officer or, indeed, just a kindly neighbour are all therapists in this sense. Furthermore, if the help is provided through psychological means (discussion, guidance, etc.) rather than chemical or financial means, then whoever is doing the helping is a psychotherapist in the widest sense of the word. It is never correct to assume that a lack of academic qualifications invalidates the therapeutic value of the help which can be provided by a particular person. Academic training assists the interviewer to recognize important processes during the course of interviewing but is not a defining criterion of a therapist. Indeed, the best therapist on the staff of one hospital for schizophrenics is an old Italian cleaning lady who, it is acknowledged, 'doesn't speak very much of the English'.

It is equally important to realize that virtually every social interaction has a strong and often definitive effect upon the behaviour, both present and future, of those involved in the interaction. There is never an occasion when change does not take place where two people interact and it is imperative that this fact is never lost sight of.

When two people interact, it is usually with a view to exchanging ideas, obtaining assistance or, more often than not, with a view to having their own opinions substantiated. An easy trap for any therapist is for him to unwittingly support the deviant ideas of a patient or client and thereby retard therapy rather than advance it. How this can be avoided is dealt with later in the chapter. A therapeutic interview is defined as any form of social interaction in which help is sought and, hopefully, received. A more appropriate term for this type of social interaction would therefore be a 'helping interview' and this is the term which will be used henceforth in this chapter when referring to any therapeutic interaction in psychotherapy and social work.

Traditions of interviewing

Traditions in interviewing can be divided into two main categories: the directive and non-directive traditions. Since interviews can be divided into those which are personal and those which are group interviews (as in Chapter I), this division of traditions can be combined with the numbers of people involved in interviewing to yield a two by two matrix table as in Figure 6. Every helping interview can be fitted into one or the other quadrants of this

	Non-directive	Directive
Individual		
Group		

FIGURE 6   *Tradition/therapy matrix*

matrix, since any helping interview must involve either individuals or groups in face to face encounters and requires the application of considerations pertaining to either the directive tradition or the non-directive (or client-centred approach, as Rogers subsequently called it).

Directive and non-directive interviewing

The philosophical views that are held by the therapist concerning the client's role obligations and the activities which should enable him to reflect these obligations, and those which define, from this, the role of the therapist, are crucial in the delineation of directive and non-directive interviewing. If the therapist subscribes to the psychoanalytic tradition (which encompasses the schools of Freud, and the schools of Neo-Freudians such as Sullivan, Horney, and the

Menninger and Tavistock Institutes), or the Rogerian or client-centred tradition, then the interview will be non-directive, since the therapist would aim at providing insight for the client into the nature and sources of his own behaviour and the reasons why his behaviour reflects psychological difficulties. If, on the other hand, the therapist subscribes to the views of Glasser, the interview will be directive. Glasser (1965), like others who subscribe to the directive tradition, considers that the aetiology of the problem and insight for the client are relatively unimportant. The important factor for him is to have the client face up to the problem as it appears at the moment of interaction with the therapist and to plan how to cope with it today, tomorrow and in the future.

The conception of the needs of the client also enters into the distinction between directive and non-directive interviews. Many people involved in the helping professions feel that the function of the therapist is to provide insight into the client's problems, but not to offer ways of resolving them. This certainly applies to adherents of the psychoanalytic tradition who consider that the aim of psychotherapy and counselling in general should be concerned with determining the aetiology of the problem in childhood and with assisting the client to obtain insight into how this problem arose. They believe that by doing so, the problem will lose its psychological impact and thus enable the client to handle it. On the other hand, adherents of the Rogerian or non-directive tradition assume that their clients are normally capable individuals who really know what they want but require a sounding board for their ideas. Accordingly, the therapist's function is to provide, and indeed become, this sounding board. As this method of counselling was designed to assist high school and university students in making up their minds about courses and careers, its inherent assumptions about the client are reasonable and understandable. High school and university students are reasonably clear about what they require from education even if they are often unclear about the courses which they should follow. It is, however, widely applied in psychotherapy and social work.

The degree of involvement allowed for the therapist by the psychoanalytic schools of thought differs from that allowed by the Rogerians, even though both schools fall within the non-directive tradition. Though the psychoanalytic school recognize the important role which the therapist must play in the whole of the counselling process, nevertheless the degree of involvement which he is allowed is less than that allowed for by the Rogerians. His role is confined to getting the client to recognize the psychological blockages, defence mechanisms and other unconscious factors which account for his behaviour. Only by recognizing these, can the client gain insight into the unconscious sources of his own behaviour. On the other hand, the Rogerians allow for a relatively greater involvement of the therapist in the counselling process not only because he must act as a sounding-board but also because he must, in so doing, recognize and respect the awareness of the client. The psychoanalytic schools assume that the client does not know or understand his own problem and that the therapist's usefulness in counselling must, in itself, depend on his trained (through psychoanalysis) ability to recognize his own psychological blockages in relation to the client. The Rogerian school assumes that the client knows his problem, understands it and can therefore resolve it himself if he is given the opportunity of discussing it with a sympathetic therapist. However, both schools of thought aim at the development of a certain degree of insight on the part of the client into his own problems. They are both firmly within the non-directive tradition of interviewing.

The directive schools of Glasser (Reality Therapy), Ellis (Rational Therapy), Carkhuff and Berenson (Eclectic) and Schutz (Gestalt), all allow for an even greater degree of involvement of the therapist than the Rogerians. They believe that the client knows his problems and that his state of awareness is not impaired by them; nevertheless, he lacks the capacity to resolve them. The therapist should therefore take an active part in helping him to resolve them.

The distinctions between the two main traditions of interviewing—directive and non-directive—are not therefore abstract distinctions but are distinctions which dictate the practical stances which both therapists and clients should adopt during the course of counselling.

The progression of counselling

A course of counselling usually involves a number of interviews spread out over a period of time. Each interview consists of a beginning, a middle or main body and an ending as we have shown in the last chapter. All three parts are closely integrated in such a way that a satisfactory beginning tends to carry over into the main body of the interview and through to the ending of the interview. Some of the skill elements that are applied to the whole interview are more relevant to the beginning than to the main body as we have shown but the explorations into the personality which are central to the therapeutic interview are largely confined to the main body of the interview. A course of counselling over a number of interviews is directed at the personality dispositions of both therapists and clients and is therefore focused largely on the main body of all the interviews which are involved.

Therapeutic interaction over a number of interviews passes, in general, through three phases. The first phase consists of the attempt by the therapist to obtain an understanding of the nature of the problems which the client experiences and to build up rapport in order to facilitate communication for the rest of the course of counselling. This may, or may not be achieved in the first interview. This phase may take up the first couple of interviews. The development of rapport is essential to the course of counselling since the client can only begin to examine the hidden depths of his own personality after his fears and apprehensions about the therapist's activities have been laid aside. The development of confidence progresses concomitantly with the development of rapport.

The second phase consists of the assessment and evaluation of the nature of the problem by the therapist. Such an assessment may not succeed in tracing the aetiology of the problem since the emphasis need not (except where the Freudian school of thought is involved) be placed on the early developmental history of the client. But any evaluation of the problem at this phase must result in an awareness of the extent to which the problem interferes with the client's adjustment. Though this second phase is distinguishable from the first, nevertheless the latter usually progresses into the former and on to the third phase.

The third phase involves the therapist in a re-structuring process, in which he aims to enable the client to become self-sufficient both as an individual and in relation to his group affiliations.

The Freudian school of thought requires that once progression through the first two phases have resulted in sufficient insight into the aetiology of the problem for both therapist and client, the client can himself be left to re-organize his personality into that of a fully functioning individual. But even in situations where no specific theoretical tradition is being consciously applied to the interview by the therapist, this third and most important phase is never successfully completed by the client on his own.

The client always begins a counselling course at a predetermined level. At the first interview, the level is determined by the client's problem, but as the course of counselling progresses, the level becomes determined by the point in the counselling programme that the client has reached. Each interview, in a counselling course, is a new ball game and not an extension of an earlier one. The initial point of entry is that marked as point 'E' in Figure 7. With the progression of the course of counselling, the functioning level of the client declines and then increases up to the final interview. Though this progression through I^2 in Figure 7 characterizes counselling in which Freudian and Neo-Freudian ideas are applied, never-

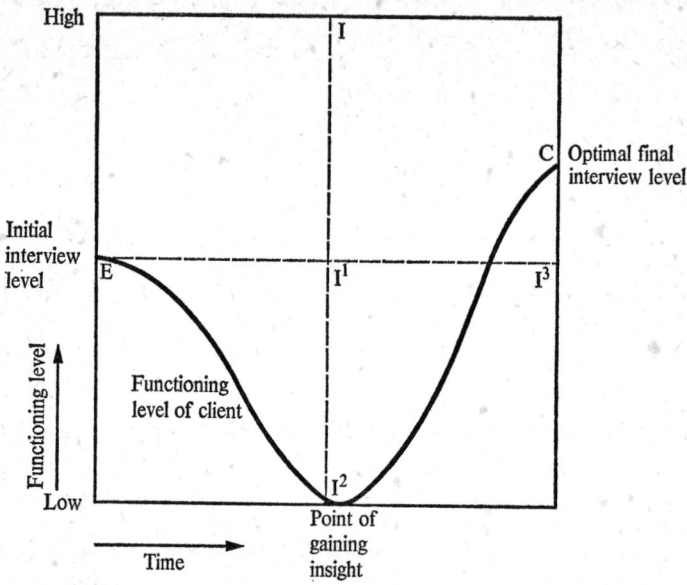

FIGURE 7 *The progression of counselling*

theless it occurs in all other therapy contexts. A certain degree of self-knowledge for the client emerges out of a therapeutic inter-action. This is most highly emphasized in 'Freudian' and 'Neo-Freudian' counselling because of their inherent theoretical rationale concerning the client. This rationale presumes that the client does not know what his problem really is, even though he may claim to know. The process of developing insight (i.e. the progression from points E to I^2) is, itself, part of the treatment, for the client can then be presumed to be able to resolve his problems. It amounts to the presumption that the problem becomes more manageable when it is no longer repressed in the subconscious. Therapists who oper-ate with a psychoanalytic frame of reference, adopt this method of operation because they believe that no problem can ever be resolved without determining its aetiology in the first place.

The search for the aetiology often takes a long time to achieve. But even where it has been achieved, a successful treatment cannot always be guaranteed as the following report in London (1964, p. 60) shows:

A Senior consultant in psychiatry in California, faced with a class of residents in psychiatry who were disturbed at the lack of progress which they were making with their patients, told the class not to be concerned about how long therapy took because 'I have seen one homosexual patient for 15 years, for ten of which he was under intensive therapy. He is now making such good progress that in about another 5 or 10 years he should be able to make a normal heterosexual adjustment.'

During the lengthy period of time which explorations into the aetiology of the problem requires, the client not only declines in his level of functioning but also becomes increasingly dependent on his therapist. At his lowest point of decline (point I^2 in Figure 7), he either obtains adequate insight into his problem or he becomes only too happy to accept whatever the therapist tells him about his problem. Usually, the non-directive or insight therapist at this point in the proceedings considers that the client now knows his problem and can understand how it arose, does not need further help and can cope with the solution himself. However, the client may, at this point, be entirely dependent upon the therapist and needs him even more than he did when he requested help at point E in Figure 7.

The recidivism rate of psychiatric patients in particular is extremely high because counselling is usually broken off at this point. The explanation put forward by the non-directive psychoanalytic therapists for this high recidivism rate is that the patient finished counselling too early and before complete insight into his problem had been achieved, or that the patient had more than one problem to deal with. This, needless to say, is rubbish: what in fact has occurred is that the client has been made completely dependent on his therapist instead of being enabled to stand on his own two feet. Where psychoanalytic insight counselling usually ends (Point I^2 Figure 7) is in fact where true counselling should really begin. The Rogerian school believes that clients know their problem and therefore start counselling at Point I^2 but do not usually raise the level of effectiveness of their clients much above Point I^3 Figure 7. Some writers (for example London) feel that the psychoanalytic insight counsellors are guilty of fraud, for they are offering help, but at best only delivering insight and often delivering nothing other than a dependency situation.

What has all this to do with traditions of interviewing you might ask. The answer is, 'Everything'. As stated earlier, there are two traditions of counselling and interviewing: insight or non-directive, and directive. When an interview is non-directive, the therapist acts as a sounding board so that the client can gain insight into his problems and be enabled to solve them himself with little assistance from the therapist. With directive counselling, the therapist takes an active part in the interview and directs the client into the appropriate course of action which he should follow. In other words, the directive therapist directs the client on to a course which will resolve the client's problem from the beginning E to I³. The aetiology of the problem is not of primary importance to the directive therapist; what is of direct importance, is that the client is receiving help on how to live with or overcome his difficulties, resolve his deviancy and function at a normal level again. The following will help to illustrate this point:

A young boy of 15 is perpetually getting into trouble with the law by shop-lifting. There is no necessity for him to steal for he always has more than sufficient money on him at the time of his commission of the offences. Apart from this, the stolen goods are seldom of any use to him and are not readily resaleable. The boy is ultimately placed on probation to a probation officer who decides that the boy has a psychiatric problem and obtains treatment for him. After many months of intensive treatment, the insight therapist concludes that because of the weaning method employed on the boy, he hates his mother and that the stealing is aimed at punishing her. The therapist conveys this information to the boy who indicates that he now fully understands why he steals and confirms that he doesn't like his mother very much. Convinced that the boy has complete insight into his problem, the therapist considers him cured and cancels further therapy. Three weeks later the boy is again before the court for stealing. When asked by his probation officer why he committed the offence, the boy replied with the authoritative excuse willingly provided by the therapist, 'It wasn't my fault, I couldn't help it. I hate my mother and I wanted to punish her'.

For all the help this insight therapist was to this boy and many others like him, it would have been better for the boy never to have seen him. All that happened was that the therapist provided the boy with a valid excuse for his behaviour, backed by the authoritative opinion of the therapist.

Unfortunately, this happens every day to the detriment of clients. The following social work example will further illustrate the inadequacies of the non-directive approach to problem solving.

A woman with 5 children was living on mother's allowance and under the care of a social worker. One day she telephoned her social worker to say that she had received an eviction notice for non-payment of rent. The social worker phoned the council who was her landlord, and was told that the woman was over 3 months in arrears with her rent. The social worker was also later told by the client that neither the rent nor the electricity had been paid for because she hadn't the money to pay them when they fell due. On going over the situation with the client, the social worker pointed out to the client that the problem was not so much concerned with a shortage of money, but was more concerned with poor budgeting. The client had now gained insight into her problem and was told by the social worker that if she were to budget properly, she would no longer have to face this problem as all her expenses would be covered. At this point the social worker promised to have the arrears paid off and departed, telling the client to set up a budget and to keep to it. The social worker, true to her word, paid off the arrears.

Two months later, the same problem came up again. When asked by the social worker how it was that the problem arose after telling the client to budget, the latter replied, 'I wanted to budget, but I do not know what you mean or how to do it'.

What was needed in this illustration was genuine help, not insight. Insight in the first illustration did nothing to help the boy to cope with his uncontrollable desire to steal; in fact, it provided him with a ready-made excuse for his deviant behaviour. In the second illustration, the mother's insight into her problem did nothing to assist her with the problem of budgeting.

But if these shortcomings are evident in psychoanalytic counselling, do they not also apply to the client-centred approach of Rogers since, after all, they are both constituents of the nondirective tradition? The answer must, most obviously, be 'Yes', for the Rogerians regard the therapist as a sounding board which could answer back if necessary within an atmosphere of unconditional and positive regard for the client. But the response of the therapist does not involve a dictation of the course of action which the client should adopt but guidance in a specific direction up to the point of accomplishment in C in Figure 7. The Rogerians do not therefore allow the therapist to be as actively involved with the client as the directive therapists do, even though they more subtly guide the client into those directions which would have the effect of restoring him to the optimal level of functioning. Rogerian therapists in the last-mentioned illustration would not therefore feel disposed to work out with the client the arithmetical elements of budgeting but they would not stop only at the point of insight, but continue along the direction of the line in Figure 7. To this extent, they attempt to go beyond the point at which psychoanalytic counselling would cease. Nevertheless, they are equally guilty of the shortcomings mentioned in relation to psychoanalytic counselling, because they do not feel impelled to be as active in the counselling process as directive therapists would be.

The contrast between therapists of the non-directive (psychoanalytic or Rogerian) and the directive schools turns sharply on the question of responsibility for the client's subsequent actions. Once one joins the ranks of directive therapists, one becomes responsible in no small measure for those one offers to help. Whatever the client does as a result of his interaction with the directive therapist becomes almost as much the responsibility of the therapist as it is of the client. To be a directive therapist, interviewer or social worker, requires that one progresses beyond the point of insight development, for it is necessary to proceed to point C irrespective of one's personal cost in terms of time or effort. No longer can one remain uninvolved and detached, for one has offered to provide help in every sense of the word; consequently one must be ready to accept responsibility for the failures as well as for the successes of one's clients in re-adjusting themselves. The responsibility rests on the therapist because he would have been the catalyst which brought about the course of action which the client is to follow. This responsibility must never be under-estimated, for the client's future behaviour depends on how well this responsibility is handled. The directive therapist does more than provide insight for the client; he actively aids the client with resolving problems as they arise. The emphasis for him is not on the reasons why a client experiences certain problems but on how he can be enabled to cope with similar problems today, tomorrow and in the future.

In the first illustration, the boy needed to be taught how to cope with his hostile feelings towards his mother. The very last thing the boy needed was a ready-made excuse for his deviant behaviour, but that, in fact, was what he got. The therapist entirely missed the point; the boy needed help, not insight. This also applied to the second illustration. The mother of five children realized that her bad budgeting was at the root of her problem even though she may not have known it by this name. What she needed was to be taught how to budget and spend her money wisely, rather than to be told in the abstract that budgeting was what she needed. The social worker should have sat down and shown her how to budget and should have taken her on at least one shopping expedition to show her how to shop wisely.

It is imperative that the client receives as much help as is humanly possible without removing the initiative for action from him. This is particularly important at the beginning of a therapeutic interaction. The client should thereafter be gradually weaned to the point where he can function on his own. This weaning process can involve as much strain on the therapist as on the client, for as the client becomes more self-sufficient, so the role of the therapist becomes increasingly unnecessary. The gradual disappearance of his function can result in strong feelings of rejection within the therapist.

A directive therapist is not only responsible for the behaviour of his clients, but is also, by virtue of this, vulnerable; he can be hurt by the client's failures in carrying out the actions which are expected of him. Unless the therapist is himself a very secure person, the failures of his clients can have serious effects on his morale. It is essential, in view of this, that the prospective student be clear in his own mind as to his motivations for wishing to enter the helping professions; he should be certain that vicarious enjoyment of other people's difficulties is not one of them; he must be equally certain that involvement in the helping professions is not merely a substitute for something else more attractive. Only where such clarification is forthcoming, can one become, in time, a secure therapist or social worker who can manage problems of transference and dependence adequately.

On the effect of the location of the interview

Feelings of dependence or rejection, the emergence of psychological crisis situations and the building up of rapport all depend only partly on the philosophical traditions which the therapist adopts during the actual course of interview. They also depend on the location of the interview.

Much has been written on the relative merits of holding interviews in the office of the therapist as against holding interviews in the home of the client. Such material is useful for indicating the extent to which one location is to be preferred to another. However, such discussions completely miss the point, for they assume that the ideal location for any interview is a matter which can be decided in an abstract and almost formal way. This is far from being the case. The determination of the ideal location for any interview cannot be decided in the abstract but depends on the reason for the therapeutic interaction in the first place.

It can therefore be asserted that, in general, an interview should be conducted in the situation which is most closely related to the problem under discussion. This, in effect, means that an interview with a crane driver who works on overhead cranes and whose problems are related to his anxieties about heights, should be conducted at the client's place of employment. The matter of choosing between the office and the home for an interview is therefore unimportant except where the problems experienced by the client are most adequately handled in an office or are related to his domestic conditions.

It is, however, not always possible to undertake counselling in the situation that produces the problem for the client. A client whose problems are connected with flying cannot be interviewed in an aircraft nor, for that matter, can an overhead crane driver always be interviewed in his place of employment. The question as to whether the home should be preferred for interviewing as against the office is therefore one which must be resolved on practical grounds rather than on the basis of abstract theory. It is in the light of practical necessities, that the relative merits of office as against home interviewing should be considered. We shall examine the practical factors which are involved in office interviewing; those which are involved in home interviewing will be dealt with at length in the next chapter.

The office interview

The most common place for holding interviews is in the office of the caseworker or therapist. This situation contributes an air of authority to the proceedings and is well suited to many types of interviewing. Unfortunately, this air of authority can create inhibitions in the interviewee. The fact that psychiatrists, psychologists, etc., use offices to see their patients is a contributory factor in the very slow build up of rapport between the therapist and patient. This must always be considered when setting a place for an interview. It is not uncommon practice in North America, for companies to interview prospective senior employees in a motel or hotel room. This, they maintain, enables the interviewer to see the prospective employee in a relaxed atmosphere, and to feel his way into the real character of the person. The author has been interviewed for jobs in North America in the homes of senior company executives for exactly this reason. An interviewer who sits behind a desk is much more likely to create inhibitions in the mind of the interviewee than one who sits comfortably in a motel room.

However, this is not always possible. What, then, can be done to break down the strained atmosphere of the office interview? The answer to this question presumes that it is easy to re-structure the office atmosphere and that it is always advisable to do so. There are situations where such re-structuring is not advisable. Where, for example, a probation officer wishes to censure a probationer for misdemeanour, it is not advisable to restructure the office atmosphere to the point where the authority of the probation officer can be seriously undermined in the mind of the client. In this case, the probation officer would want to reflect as much authority to the probationer as possible. He would therefore have the probationer sit in front of his desk while he sits behind it. This position of interviewer and interviewee provides physical distance between the two and prevents any kind of physical contact; the desk constitutes a symbol of authority which would clearly reinforce the roles of the two characters. The necessary censure can then be carried out by the probation officer, using the desk and the relative positions of himself and his client as symbols of his authority.

Having carried out the censure, the probation officer may then wish to get on more friendly terms with his client. To do this, the probation officer would abandon his position behind his desk and take a seat alongside or close to his client in front of the desk. With the desk no longer a barrier between them, a more friendly atmosphere will develop in which the more personal problems of the client can be explored.

This switching of positions is an important means by which the atmosphere of an interview can be changed, particularly when some action which may be unpleasant to both parties has to be carried out before more pleasant ones can be dealt with. Where there are a number of possible seating arrangements in an office, the choice of the client as to where and how he sits should be carefully noted for they can tell a great deal more about his moods and needs than the communication which is exchanged during the actual course of the interview. Even where there is only one possible seating arrangement in an office, much can be learnt from the way the client takes his seat, for it will show the therapist if he is friendly, hostile, depressed or just annoyed at having to turn up for the appointment. Such information can be useful in deciding on the approach which should be adopted in building up rapport.

The layout and decor of an office can change or influence the outcome of an interview. This should be considered when furnishing and decorating an office. A room which looks austere and forbidding to the client can make it difficult for rapport to be established. On the other hand, the austerity with which an office is decorated and the seating arrangements which are provided within it, can influence the degree of authority which the therapist will reflect to the client. For example, the office of a probation officer should be warm and friendly but, at the same time, be authoritarian, whereas the office of a clinical psychologist should be relaxing and mildly authoritarian.

However, the author has practised as a clinical psychologist for a number of years and prefers, on the basis of his experience, to interview patients in their own homes whenever this is possible.

The quickest results can be obtained by using this location. Nevertheless, it is incorrect to assume that an office interview must necessarily fail or that the office of a therapist or social worker must necessarily be so forbidding and austere as to impose a negative influence on the progression of counselling or interviewing.

Group interviewing: practical problems

So far, the discussion has ignored the group interviewing situation and its associated practical problems. The first problem in such a situation is that the interviewer is outnumbered and that the members of the group can 'gang up' on the interviewer if they feel threatened. How big this problem is depends on the personality of the interviewer and on his skill in breaking up this unconsciously contrived 'conspiracy'. Some interviewers can cope with this problem in an easy and relaxed way while others go to pieces. It is important therefore to use the interviewing situation which best suits the interviewer rather than the clients, but every effort should be made by the interviewer to develop a technique for handling group interviews.

The group interview is particularly useful, for it permits social interaction to occur in front of the interviewer which would otherwise be hidden from him. This is particularly true of psychiatric patients and young offenders who may be scapegoats for other people. The more insight the interviewer can acquire into the current situation surrounding the client, the easier it is to provide assistance for the client in coping with such a situation.

The problem of controlling the proceedings of a group interview while allowing every member an opportunity to speak openly should never be under-estimated. In some cases, clients are afraid to express their views in the presence of other group members; consequently the interviewer has to pry out virtually every word from the clients. In other cases, one or two group members may attempt to dominate the entire proceedings and thereby prevent free expression by other members. In view of these possibilities, it is necessary for the interviewer to take a strong hold on the proceedings so that every member can have an opportunity.

When a group enters a room, special note should be made of where each member sits and who sits next to whom, for this will provide clues as to the group's construction and who supports whom. If one member is left to sit alone while the others form a group, then this is an indication that he is the group's scapegoat. Generally, it is important to identify the significant others that a client interacts with, and the nature of that interaction, because no man operates in a vacuum. To resolve a client's problems usually involves doing something about his environment and those with whom he interacts in an intimate way. This usually requires the therapist to deal with the family of the client and to sort out whatever problems impinge on the client's behaviour from that source. This may often bring the therapist into conflict with various factions of the client's family as he is often seen as an intruder into their private domain. Members of the family may constantly change sides from being for him to being against him. They may also express their hostility overtly. A family using one of its members as a scapegoat can become very hostile when their negative use of that individual is pointed out to them.

This hostility can be skilfully exploited by the therapist to elicit the family's true feelings and emotions. Hostility can, in this way, be put to constructive use by the therapist. In any case, it is one of the responsibilities of the therapist to ensure that hostilities within the family are handled constructively rather than destructively. The observation of family conflicts and their resolution can be best carried out in the family's usual place of residence or in an atmosphere approximating to it. This is one reason why the author sometimes uses his own living-room for therapy, for it provides a relaxed and comfortable atmosphere with plenty of space for clients to position themselves as they would do in their own homes. The author attributes much of his success with adolescents, children and families to his not using an office.

The positions that members of a family or group take up relative to each other at an interview constitute a non-verbal form of communication and should be carefully noted for they indicate, in a relatively clear way, the authority hierarchy and the blue-print of friendliness within it. This can tell the interviewer more about the family or group than he can learn from a dozen interviews where only the verbal aspects of communication are noted.

To touch or not to touch

Professional ethics tell us that we should never touch our clients and yet a simple act like taking someone's hand can say more than a book. The strength that can be given to a client by placing one's arm around them in times of stress or by holding their hand is immeasurable. The touch of a hand can show more concern and compassion than can ever be expressed verbally. Our language unfortunately is not over-abundant in expressions of emotional tenderness and to express them usually requires another medium. The only medium that we really have at our disposal is that of touch and this should be used spontaneously whenever it is appropriate. It should never be used in a calculated way for it then becomes what it is not. Harlow (1958) using monkeys and Schutz (1969) using humans, show the full extent to which tactile contact is important. This topic is covered in an excellent book by Schutz which is highly recommended reading for all those involved in the helping professions.

We can now summarize the important points which have emerged from our discussion in this chapter.

It is true to say that the Rogerian and the psychoanalytic non-directive approaches to counselling are not particularly effective, partly because they often involve lengthy operations and partly because they may unwittingly provide supportive excuses for vacil-lation or for the deviant behaviour of clients. The directive ap-proach, on the other hand, has the drawback of requiring the therapist to reduce his detachment at some point and to commit himself to directing his clients' behaviour and taking responsibility for the ultimate outcome of therapeutic interaction. This is very often the case in psychotherapy.

The demands made upon the directive therapist are many; they include directness, honesty and frankness. They require him to make moral judgments which may be based on his own biases. He must help the client to face up to reality and to make plans for the future. He must also aid the client in fulfilling the aims of treatment which both he and the client will have established jointly. He must also ensure that these aims are realistic. In view of his responsibility for the outcome of therapeutic interaction on the behaviour of the client, he would not advise deviant behaviour as a matter of policy but may recognize that the client's problems some-times require a contravention of society's mores (in relation to sexual matters for example). He must therefore expect and be willing to accept criticism from other members of the helping professions who may accuse him of playing God and of manipu-lating the lives of his clients.

However, the results that can be obtained by directive therapy more than compensate for the demands and responsibilities which are placed on the directive therapist. Professional detachment is impossible to maintain throughout the three phases of the counsel-ling process, even though it is important at the beginning of the initial interview. As counselling progresses further into the other phases, subjective feelings and spontaneous responses become as important as is objective observation of the client's reactions.

8

Interviewing in special situations

All social situations involve and revolve around people. The interview situation, particularly, is a highly personal experience involving a direct confrontation between two or more individuals. The interviewer rarely has prior knowledge of his prospective client, and he is never in a position to select those whom he will interview. He is therefore left with only the skills of his training and the strengths and weaknesses of his own personality, to face the variety of highly idiosyncratic individuals who come and confront him not only with their problems and shortcomings but, often more frequently than is comfortable, with his own.

There are no short cuts to success; there is no easy way of categorizing the multiplicity of different personalities into convenient types which can be dealt with by the production of the appropriate punch-card. The professional interviewer must take on all comers in the total certainty that each will be different and that there is no such thing as a stock response to a stock type.

However, the fact that there is no such creature as the stock interviewee or the stock client does not preclude the argument that there are basic types of interviewing situations which are commonly experienced in social work and which impose demands on the social worker's basic ability to deal with human beings. The pressure of these demands can make life problematic for the social worker. This chapter examines a number of basic interviewing situations and illustrates their problematic elements.

As has been stated earlier, there is always an element of role reversal between participants. Both sides switch from being the interviewee to being the interviewer and back again, often with bewildering rapidity. This is necessary not only to facilitate the interchange of communication, but also to allow both sides to gain insight into the deeper aspects of each other's character.

However, there comes a stage beyond this when a sense of panic indicates that control is lost; the interviewee is dominant and the only fact of which the interviewer feels certain is his inadequacy to deal with the personality and problems facing him.

Two basic causes for this often unnecessary rout and destruction of ego and confidence are, first, relative inexperience and second, a sense of isolation. The typewriter or the computer with which the mature entrant to the social work field may well have had his sole experience of formal one-to-one interviewing, is poor preparation for dealing with the many multi-faceted personalities who confront him six months or a year later. The veneer of confidence and expertise inculcated by training can quickly crack under bombardment from a constant stream of deranged or demanding personalities.

How reassuring it would be to know that the fully-trained and apparently imperturbable caseworker in the office next door also meets with equally demoralizing experiences, but knows how to handle such situations both to his own and to his clients' advantage.

The following empirical illustrations of interviewing situations are presented as much for reassurance as for learning. They are drawn from casework notes. They will reflect differences based on the individual personalities of those who were directly involved, but these illustrations touch on basic situations which can often arise throughout the social worker's professional life.

Interviewing in the home: practical issues

There are four basic causes for home interviewing. The first concerns the need to relate the client's personality and problems to the domestic background which he enjoys (or suffers from as the case may be) and, from this, to see whether it is the client alone who requires the social worker's assistance or whether his individual problems merely reflect common problems within his family background. This is, in the first instance at least, a straightforward fact-finding exercise which could be useful for the social worker's evaluation of the client's problems or for the information of a court of law.

A second cause for home interviewing concerns the desire of a social worker to broaden his perspective on a client who is already well known in the office interview situation and for whom, one feels, the time has come to enlarge one's acquaintance and meet the whole family.

A third cause for home interviewing concerns the routine home visit to a client who may find it inconvenient to attend at the office. Such a client could be a mother who is known to leave children alone and who would certainly leave them if she had to journey to the office.

A fourth cause for home interviewing is more directly concerned with the social condition of a family. Crisis situations can arise within families which are already known to the social worker which could demand his entry into a completely unknown home and family situation.

A further reason for home interviewing concerns the ease with which rapport can be established. This has been touched upon in the last chapter and will not therefore receive consideration here.

Two fundamentals have to be faced on all home visits. First, one must ensure that the purpose of the visit is clearly understood and second, one must overcome the potential problem of the television set. These fundamentals are interrelated.

The appearance of the social worker in the living room means that the favourite television programme of at least one person present will undoubtedly have been interrupted. It is very important to appreciate this. For example, in a situation where one child is delinquent because he is made the scapegoat for all the ills that befall the family, the cause of that child's integration and acceptance is hardly likely to be furthered by the destruction of an evening's viewing.

On a fact-finding mission, where one or more members of the family have broken the rules of social behaviour and placed themselves in a position where their liberty could be restricted by law, it is not unreasonable for the social worker or the Probation Officer to request either that the television be switched off, or that the interview with those directly concerned be held in another room if, that is, there is another room.

The reaction to either suggestion, however, depends not only on how socially responsible the family is, but also on how well the purpose of the visit has been explained and how well the terms of reference for the interview have been established. Your identity must be quickly established and the purpose of your visit clearly explained. At any one time, a family in a state of social breakdown may be expecting visits from the 'electricity man', the 'gas board man', the 'tallyman', or the landlord—expectations which are unlikely to be advantageous to the conduct of the interview. Your carefully worded letter of introduction may have been misappropriated by another tenant on the 'first come first claimed' principle which so often applies to post arriving in a multi-tenanted house. It may have been mislaid, misunderstood, or just frankly ignored, in the vain hope that if it is not in any way acknowledged, the sender may never arrive.

Success in establishing communication and rapport can often be judged by the speed with which the television is turned down or switched off. If the set is allowed to take precedence, the message is either that you have not clearly explained the purpose of your visit, or that you have not established your goodwill. If this week's thrilling instalment is allowed to grind inexorably and loudly on, resist the temptation either to join the viewing circle or to turn the set off yourself, but start again by explaining the reason for your presence.

When the social worker is a frequent and well-known visitor to the household, inclusion in the family viewing circle or an invitation to stay for dinner may not only be something of a compliment but can also provide a useful opportunity to observe natural family group interaction.

Aside from the influence of television, the room chosen for the interview and the behaviour the parents permit to those other members of the family who are present, but not directly concerned, are useful indications of how outside authority figures are regarded. Even the disposition of family pets, particularly if these are large dogs, can provide the social worker with food for thought and the germ of a casework plan on what might, at first sight, appear to be a fruitless and perhaps potentially dangerous home visit.

It is not uncommon in a crowded urban society, for one child of a respectable law-abiding family to become involved in an offence. The family may feel embarrassed by it. In such circumstances, it is important that the intervention of the social worker should be seen as bringing some advantage to the whole family if a scapegoating situation is to be prevented. It should not be used as a constant reminder of their public and private disgrace.

An example is David, a 16-year-old apprentice motor mechanic who had allowed his enthusiasm for cars to involve him in the removal of an 'old banger' from a nearby kerb. The head of the family was the grandfather. He was a morally upright, somewhat despotic old man, with a passion for racing pigeons. The rest of the family did not share his interest and the old man's despotism in the home contained an element of compensation for the family's lack of interest in his hobby. The hours spent in the pigeon loft, with the birds zooming past our heads, gave the old man an opportunity to talk about his hobby to an outsider who appeared to be genuinely interested. Home visits invariably gravitated towards the pigeon loft where, with the birds zooming about, the old man had the opportunity of talking about his hobby.

By his offence, David had indeed brought notoriety to the family but he had also unknowingly provided its most influential member with an interested audience. It was therefore difficult for the grandfather to believe that the consequences of the boy's misdemeanour were wholly bad and a situation was avoided which might have led David to leave home before he was sufficiently mature.

Interviewing the mentally ill

The concept of community care for the mentally ill means that the social worker is frequently responsible for people who, until comparatively recently, would have been confined to a mental hospital. Society's insistence that the Courts deal with an offender only after paying due regard to his mental condition means that a number of mentally and behaviourally unstable people are often consigned to the care of the social worker. A potentially disturbing experience may therefore be in store for the social worker who has had little psychiatric training.

Whether the interview takes place in the home, the office or the prison cell, the main thing to remember is that you are sane. The mentally ill will use their illness as a defence when the interview moves on to ground that is painful, in much the same way as anyone will use either some aspect of their personality, or some personal circumstance, as a defence when the subject-matter of the interview becomes unpleasant.

There is little difference in motivation between the adolescent who threatens to 'get my mates to do yer over' and the paranoid schizophrenic who launches into a weird tale about his empathy with superhuman forces. The depressive who immediately withdraws in upon himself and pulls down his personal shutters, is responding no differently from the neglectful housewife who keeps her front door firmly closed against all inspection.

The approach, in the case of a schizophrenic who immediately becomes confused and threatening, is to keep in touch with reality. Refer back to a simple and, if possible, not too unpalatable fact which both sides have already acknowledged as factual and real, and refuse to be caught up in his flight to the wilder shores of fantasy. If one incontrovertible fact that both sides accept can be established, the client will often recognize not only that you expect a degree of lucidity, but that you also believe that the client is capable of rational thought processes.

For instance, a latent schizophrenic comes to the office by bus. This is casually established in discussion when you collect him from the waiting room. Later in the interview, when the conversation begins to move in the direction of fantasy, reference to this one non-threatening fact can distract the client from his apprehensions about the subject under discussion and prevent a defensive flight into fantasy.

At worst, your insistence on the one point that you both know is real may prevent the sort of outburst that too often causes the ignominious flight of the social worker down the garden path, or the summoning of the police to the office to deal with behaviour that has gone beyond the bounds of acceptability. Neither of these responses is really conducive to the development of a good relationship which, after all, is what the interview situation is all about.

An example is Frank, who is a schizophrenic and a huge man with a history of periodic outbursts of violence, the last of which consigned his victim, a total stranger, to hospital and brought Frank before the Court. In Frank's case, violence arises out of pressure from his parents when Frank is not contributing to the family's income. This usually occurs when Frank has lost one of his many casual jobs and has not sought the Supplementary Benefit to which his mental health entitles him.

The onset of schizophrenia occurred late in Frank's teens and he had, by then, been indoctrinated into the aspiring middle class virtue of keeping appointments. However, when he did not like the object of the appointment he was always at least half an hour late; this was his non-verbal way of communicating his feelings.

Frank, now in his twenties, had a tendency to regress to childishness, and it was felt important that contact should take place in the office and away from the home to emphasize Frank's adult, independent identity. Once in the office, Frank would become extremely vague when an unpleasant subject was broached. He would be vague not only about the subject under discussion, but about his identity, and even about my identity. The one constant, established fact that we were in agreement about, however, was where he lived.

Reference to the home, when Frank began to become 'fanciful', injected an element of reality into the conversation which he could accept, and forestalled the danger of further confusion leading to violence.

Frank finally reached the stage where he was calmly able to carry through a correct claim for Supplementary Benefit. An interview was also arranged with a Sheltered Workshop where Frank could earn a regular weekly wage. In the event, Frank turned up half an hour late for that interview. Clearly, the whole thing was going too fast for him, even though we had by then achieved so much progress without incident.

Timing and perception are especially important when interviewing the mentally ill. Lack of either may have the effect of making a client's thought processes appear to be less rational than they really are.

Stanley is an example. He is an extremely pallid and withdrawn schizophrenic whose condition manifested itself some ten years ago when he was in his teens. He is the only child of elderly parents and his mother went back to work so that he could be sent to a private school where he was pushed to the limits of his academic ability. He started work in a draughtsman's office where neither his work nor his behaviour drew any particular comment until his mental breakdown.

When Stanley's illness was confirmed, his father withdrew even further into his own private affairs. His mother became embittered and deeply resentful that her son had rewarded her sacrifices on his behalf by developing a severe mental illness. There was very little verbal communication at all in the house, and when his mother vented her feelings against him, Stanley would respond by pinching and physically terrorizing her. The whole atmosphere was one of withdrawal and calm hostility.

Stanley spent several periods as a voluntary patient in a large mental hospital, but during one of his spells at home, he was convicted of indecent exposure and a Probation Officer's report on him was requested. As the Court clearly felt that on this occasion Stanley had been responsible for his behaviour, it was necessary to interview him and attempt to ascertain his attitudes to society and to himself.

Although the method he used to break the law was distasteful, the offence indicated that Stanley was painfully aware of his social isolation and that he wished to make contact. Verbal communication, however, was a different matter. Our first attempt was useless. A very frightened and guilty Stanley would not say a word for a long time; he then volunteered one or two remarks which had nothing to do with the subject then under discussion.

Our second meeting arose out of a chance encounter at the mental hospital. Because our meeting was unexpected, both Stanley and I were more relaxed. Until then, I had been calling Stanley by his surname, but I now asked him if I could use his forename, and asked what it was. There was no reply and I went on with what was apparently a one-sided conversation, until he suddenly said, 'Stanley'. Had it not been a name, the connection would probably have gone unnoticed, but I recognized it as the answer to my first question. It occurred to me that Stanley might in fact be answering, but taking an abnormally long time to do so. Up to a point, this proved to be the case. Stanley would take the question right into himself; regard it from all possible angles, taste, touch and probably even smell it. If, after this thorough scrutiny, he felt that no threat was implied, he would answer. No reply probably meant that the question had failed to pass his private test of acceptability.

An indication of the degree of control Stanley had over his behaviour was obtained by this painfully slow method and relayed to the Court. Stanley was eventually allowed to continue as a voluntary mental patient at a local hospital without any legal restriction.

Interviewing the violent client

The situation where violence will occur if a sum of money, spacious accommodation or a complete change in the order of things to the client's total advantage is not forthcoming, is frequently encountered by the professional interviewer. Indeed, it is a fairly standard ingredient of his working life. The client may either be threatening violence against himself, or against you, the interviewer. Either is a situation which can cause fear and consternation.

In such circumstances, the threat of violence is being used because the client has been hurt and his only way of obtaining relief is to hurt someone else in turn. His life experience may have taught him that actual or threatened violence is the most effective way to achieve his ends.

It is difficult to generalize, particularly in the case of the casual caller who is threatening suicide, but there are certain responses which take the heat out of the situation. The likelihood of the client carrying out his threat is decreased if he is not forced into a situation where he sees no other alternative, or if the interviewer deals with the situation in such a way that the execution of the threat is clearly seen to be futile.

If the interviewer disguises his fear and makes it plain that intimidation will not produce the desired result, the client will often gratefully seize any avenue which is presented for retreat. If the interview is taking place in the office, the process of summoning a colleague may make the client feel that he is not so much the attacker as the attacked, and he will respond appropriately in his own defence. The small woman who can be subdued only by five hefty men is a case in point, and precipitating cases of Actual Bodily Harm is hardly within the social worker's brief.

Empirical experience indicates that any continuation of work with the violent client lies in the interviewer's ability to acknowledge the threat and to make it plain to the client that he will not achieve his ends in this way. The interviewer should try and make it clear that he will not be thrown off balance by such an approach, and an effective way of doing this is to return to the subject under discussion from a rational and more realistic angle.

Mr McConkey, a man in his thirties, established a claim on a particular office on the flimsiest of pretexts and then proceeded, by his physical size, his drunkenness and his threats, to terrorize various members of the staff into meeting his demands for cash and other material assistance. In Mr McConkey's case, this was not helpful, but rather perpetuated his problem of finding his own place in society.

The day came, as Mr McConkey walked truculently up the stairs, when he had to be faced not only with the reality of his behaviour as it adversely affected himself, but also with the fact that the source of ready cash had dried up.

His opening demand was for a new suit in which to attend an interview for work. The implication was that he could hardly be held responsible for his failure to obtain the job if the clothes, or a small contribution in cash, were not forthcoming.

The clothes that he was wearing were inspected and pronounced suitable for the cause. He was then asked about his qualifications for the post in question. Mr McConkey paused and, in reply, launched into a graphic description of his various convictions and his inability to control his temper when frustrated. This account was received and commented upon in a way that made it plain that the threatening implications had been clearly understood, but there was no reaction other than to return to the subject of his qualifications for the job in hand. Mr McConkey, always willing to provide a second opportunity to get his own way, then turned to the question of his need for shoes. The refusal, the threatening process and the acknowledgment were repeated.

It is difficult to be precise as to how appropriate acknowledgment of a threat can be made. One way of doing this is by listening and often by querying a veiled statement relating to violence and by asking the client for clarification. Another way is to wait until the client has finished his attempt to browbeat before returning to the subject under discussion.

This response, in Mr McConkey's case, produced a somewhat noisy retreat down the stairs and the threat that he would never come to that office again for help. He never returned. Perhaps he moved on to fresh fields and pastures new, but maybe this firm refusal to be browbeaten helped towards some change in the man himself. At least, the particular episode did not end in capitulation and the reinforcement of those traits which are least likely to help Mr McConkey find acceptance in any society. Most important perhaps for interviewee and interviewer, the response did not precipitate another conviction for violence.

It is frightening to be faced with violence and it takes calmness to deny the client, particularly the client who is threatening suicide, the anticipated response of capitulation to unwarranted and unreasonable demands. If the knife or the pills are subsequently used, with whom will the responsibility for such actions really rest? With the interviewer for his lack of circumspection in failing to identify a real, as opposed to an empty, threat or with the client

145

himself? These are questions which the social worker has to face from time to time.

It is vital that the interviewer maintains his composure where threats of violence are concerned, for his sensitivity and perception are of the utmost importance. His calmness is equally important where suicide threats are concerned. Here the operational maxim must be—to be aware of but not to show fear.

The importance of allowing the client a conversational avenue down which he can escape after having had his threats successfully parried has already been mentioned. It is equally important to provide a physical avenue along which he can escape with his hurt pride. It is important therefore not to interview the potentially violent client in an office that is cluttered up, so cluttered up that a wild gesture by the client might cause him to knock something over and become more agitated. A claustrophobic atmosphere is, in any case, unlikely to encourage calmness in a potentially violent client. Above all, never get between the client and the door so that he can rush out, if he wants to, without knocking you over.

When violence is threatened during a home interview, it is wise to leave calmly and politely before matters get out of hand, but in the office where the interviewer is on his home ground, the advantage is with him. There are many aggrieved Borstal lads with whom one would not knowingly walk down a dark alley, but the possibility of threats being turned into actual assault is vastly decreased in an office, and where the lad is confronted by an ostensibly unruffled listener.

One of my greatest compliments came from such a client who, as he left the office at the end of a stormy but bloodless session, said in a rather puzzled way, 'But I really came in 'ere to do yer over.'

Interviewing in a custodial setting

Imprisonment often places the prisoner in an emotional situation with which he is unfamiliar. His life experiences would not have taught him how to deal with such a situation. He must therefore develop an emotional defence if he is to survive it. The middle class first offender may have to become a hermit if he is to overcome the total lack of privacy. 'I asked for my own cell and it's not so bad when I'm locked up' is a common remark. The opposite type is the offender from the large family living in crowded conditions, who has to come to terms with being locked in a cell for twelve or more hours per day with only his personal thoughts to fall back on. Most prisoners, therefore, have to create a personal defence system to enable them to withstand the prison situation.

It is important for the interviewer to appreciate that the man he knew 'outside' is not going to be the same as the man he now sees in the prison. Equally, the man he gets to know in the prison is going to change when he comes out.

For the prisoner, there are two types of interviewers. First, the interviewer from 'outside' who brings not only the dust from the outside world on his feet, but also reassurance, by his very presence, that the prisoner still has an existence in that outside world. The second type of interviewer works in the prison itself and is not only seen to have as little an existence in the outside world as the prisoner has himself, but also shares the same frustrations and impotence. For example, the prison welfare officer does have access to the telephone but, like the prisoner, he does not have the liberty to go and check the welfare of the prisoner's ailing child or family.

The prisoner—and in this context the words 'prison' and 'prisoner' refer to the inmates of all custodial institutions—is very aware of the category to which a particular interviewer belongs.

The prison-based interviewer can generally be seen on request; therefore, if something is left unsaid today, it can be discussed tomorrow. However, the prospect of a visit from an outside social worker is looked forward to with great anticipation. The first priority, therefore, if you wish to avoid the risk of a chilly reception, is to arrive as punctually as possible. While you may have been battling with the distractions of the journey to the prison, the inmate may have been anxiously waiting with little to distract him except the growing conviction that you are probably not going to come after all. There is bound to be some reaction to a late arrival and it is hardly surprising if it takes the form of a defensive anger which then has to be worked through before the conversation can proceed on to a more useful plane.

It is equally important to allow sufficient time for the interview. The inmate has thought out in advance the questions and topics he wishes to raise, and it is a source of great frustration if the interview is rushed or if something important is forgotten. Time spent discussing trivialities or even in silence is not wasted if it gives the interviewee the opportunity to review the more serious matters that have been covered and remember the one vital question that he has missed but wanted to raise.

Try also to round off the interview. For example, a woman prisoner has to be told that her child has to be taken into care. This is a highly emotive situation, calling forth strong feelings of guilt; invariably, her first reactions are of resistance and anger. The resistance can be met by pointing out the lack of feasible alternatives, but it is also important to allow the anger to run its course before the interview is ended. The interviewer should try not to leave until a situation of calm, if not happiness, has been achieved. If possible, he should not leave until the conversation has shifted on to more forward-looking topics. In this case, it could be plans for re-uniting the family when the woman is released.

The interviewee who is left in a frustrated and emotional state at the end of an interview, has very few outlets in prison on which he can safely vent his feelings. The alternatives are to 'smash up', to 'cut up' or to develop such a strong defence against any emotional involvement in the future, that the chances of a successful rehabilitation are greatly decreased. One result of this state of affairs is that the client may write an angry and hostile letter to the social worker concerned.

The circumstances of a prison interview are often more distracting for the interviewer than they are for the interviewee. There may be delays and confusion before the prisoner is found; the interview may have to take place either on the wing, surrounded by activity and noise, or in full view in one of a number of glass boxes. Notwithstanding all the distractions, it is essential that the interviewer maintains his concentration. This is necessary in order that the interview may proceed without giving ground for misunderstanding and without anything being said that can possibly be construed as a promise which is not later fulfilled.

The prisoner may feel that, in order to keep your interest and, more importantly, your presence, he must appear to understand when in fact he does not. If the interviewer does not appreciate this, later confusion may be out of all proportion to the original stimulus which created it. If there is any fact of real importance to communicate, or if attitudes and principles are under discussion, it is advisable to go over the ground again and again to leave as little room as possible for misunderstanding. Accurate communication is of course important in any interview but it is even more essential in the prison setting where, once the social worker has left, clarification of an ambiguous point cannot be easily obtained.

Finally, the prison situation is one where the interview can often be usefully continued by letter. When the prisoner is no longer in the prison, the last thing he will probably have time for is a lengthy correspondence with his social worker. Indeed, as mentioned earlier, he may well prefer to ignore any written communication. However, in prison, he will often commit himself to paper, and anxiously await a reply. Three weeks may pass in a flash for the busy social worker, but for the prisoner they are twenty-one separate days. For this reason, it is essential that the reply should be promptly dealt with if correspondence is to assist the relationship which had been established by personal contact.

This section has tended to concentrate on the impact on the

prisoner of the interviewer from outside because he does have a far greater impact than that of the prison-based social worker. 'My Probation Officer' and 'My Welfare Officer' become very important people indeed when the client is confined to an institution. This importance may not (and if the client is healthy, should not) survive the return to freedom but the degree of sensitivity shown by the social worker can have a significant effect on the client's eventual adaptation to freedom.

In conclusion, the human animal is said to take some twenty-five years before his psychological maturation can be said to be complete, and before he can be reasonably expected to handle every contingency on the basis of his own past life experiences. But irrespective of the length of time which maturation requires, only a secure and fully developed personality can hope to face all the contingencies which can arise in connection with interviewing in all situations. The practical considerations that have been advanced in this chapter reflect one worker's experiences in the field. However, there are a number of equally common-place interviewing situations which have not been dealt with here but in connection with which some knowledge is important. Interviewing situations involving drug addicts, alcoholics, very young children and sexual deviants all impose different demands on the maturity and sense of security of an interviewer. The so-called 'inadequates' in modern society all impose their equally important demands on the social work interviewer who must, in order to cope, be encouraged to read on. The advice at this point is therefore that the gentle reader reads on. Additional reading material is appended to facilitate this.

9

Role play: a training technique

The last chapter provided illustrations of a number of interviewing situations which make strong demands on the interviewer's alertness and security of self. These are common situations which are often experienced by many social workers throughout their professional lives. Long exposure to such situations can create a certain degree of awareness on the part of the interviewer which enables him to recognize and deal with the challenges which they pose.

However, while practical experience in the art of interviewing is important in the development of skills, it is never sufficient. Training in the technical aspects of interviewing is also important in so far as it enables the prospective interviewer to recognize such situations and the challenges which they pose. An important training technique for interviewers is usually referred to as role playing. In this chapter, we turn our attention to role playing and its use as a technique for developing and applying some of the skill elements in interviewing which were discussed in Chapters 6 and 7.

Role playing has a long pedigree, primarily in the theories of American sociologists and psychologists. It is sometimes referred to as game simulation in psychology—a term which reflects the ideas of social psychologists like George Herbert Mead and Charles Cooley. One of the most influential psychologists to apply it to the field of counselling was Moreno in whose hands it was referred to as 'psychodrama', reflecting its implicit dramaturgical perspective. However, it is now widely used in areas of endeavour far removed from sociology and psychology, largely because it provides an opportunity for individuals to experience the emotional elements involved in taking on roles which are normally unavailable to them. It provides a means of enabling students to gain some understanding of the states of feelings of individuals who occupy a number of diverse roles in society within the context of the laboratory or within the confines of a training establishment.

Role playing is now widely used within psychotherapy as an aid to counselling. Each subject in a role play is asked to take the part of a particular character and to act out the sorts of behaviour which such a character would normally exhibit. Given the appropriate settings, individuals who are asked to play particular roles usually consciously attempt to emulate the actions normally associated with such roles, but sooner or later find that the demands of these roles are absorbed into their own personal identities. In this way, these individuals come to see themselves not as separate and independent identities from those inherent in the roles which they are asked to play, but as the real incumbents of those roles. A number of illustrations can be drawn to show how this operates in practice. In matrimonial counselling, it could be necessary to request a wife who is obsessed by the amount of time which her millionaire husband spends away from the matrimonial home, to play the role of a jet-set tycoon who is responsible for a multi-million pounds expenditure every day and vice versa. Within the field of family counselling, parents may be requested to adopt the role of their teenage daughters and vice versa. In these examples, the persons requested to play particular roles often consider themselves as 'acting' without any physical involvement, until the progression of the role play increases their psychological involvement in the roles which they thought they were 'playing'. Indeed, role playing can be a useful technical aid in training, only to the extent that participants can be encouraged to let go of their individual identities and dissolve them into those inherent in the roles they play.

We are less concerned with the theoretical pedigree of role playing in psychology and sociology in this chapter. We are more concerned with describing the results of the use of role playing in a training course for probation officers. This course was held with experienced probation officers under the leadership of two psychologists. One leader was a psychologist with a background in the non-directive tradition and the other was a psychologist with a background in the directive tradition of interviewing. This chapter describes the results of the application of role play and shows that, first, the background traditions of the psychologists who acted as leaders had effects on the composition and structure of groups and second, that role playing provides a unique opportunity for prospective (and indeed experienced) interviewers to observe their own performance of this role, as well as to take on and experience the inherent obligations of clients—a situation not normally available to them in their professional roles.

Rationale

The rationale for including role playing in the training course for probation officers was to provide them with a structured and supervised experience in interviewing in a situation in which adverse effects on clients could not possibly arise. We have stressed earlier that the therapeutic interaction which occurs within psychotherapy and social work can have lasting effects on both interviewer and clients. An untrained interviewer who is exposed to a client could unwittingly involve himself in a situation which he has not learned to handle with 'imaginative sympathy'; failure in this endeavour could affect his morale just as much as his interaction with a disturbed client could have serious effects on the latter's subsequent behaviour. In view of this, it was felt necessary to provide an opportunity within the training course for students to experience the emotional elements that are operative in an interview situation in a context which was less stressful than would be the case in an actual interview and in which the student's performance could not have any detrimental effect on clients.

In order to provide students with an opportunity of evaluating their own and each other's performance, the practice interviews were relayed through closed-circuit television equipment and stored on video-tape. This, it was hoped, would allow students not only to observe and understand some of the common errors and problematic situations which could arise in actual interviewing, but would also assist them to avoid such errors, to recognize problematic situations before they arise, and to respond to such situations in a positive way in the future. Since all the students who participated in the evaluation of video-taped material also participated earlier in the role playing sessions, they were also able to assess the way in which their colleagues in their groups viewed them. Such an opportunity for observing how other participants in the interviewing process view the interviewer is not usually available under normal working conditions since one can hardly expect realistic responses from clients as to how well the interviewer performed during the course of the interview. This proved to be one of the most valuable aspects of the entire exercise.

Students

The students who participated in the training course are probation officers with two to ten years' practical experience. Thirty-seven of them were involved, comprising fifteen females and twenty-two males, with an age range of twenty-five to fifty years. For the purpose of the role playing exercises, they were divided into three groups of nine each, and one group of ten. These groups were identified as groups A, B, C and D. Groups A and B consisted of four males and five females each while group C consisted of seven males and two females; group D consisted of seven males and three females.

Each group was selected by a group organizer but these organizers withdrew when the role playing exercises began since they were senior members of the college whose presence, it was felt, might inhibit the free expression of emotions by students during the course of the exercises. For the students to experience the emotional involvements inherent in the role playing exercises, it was essential that they reacted spontaneously to the stimuli presented by their colleagues and did not feel that senior members of the college were observing their performances with a view to relaying these to their various agencies.

The role playing exercises were led by two psychologists. One psychologist had a background in the non-directive tradition of interviewing and was responsible for groups A and B while the second had a background in the directive tradition and was responsible for groups C and D. This division of responsibility between two trained psychologists with different backgrounds was essential for assessing the subsequent effects of their backgrounds on the composition and interaction of the various groups. There are, as has been demonstrated in an earlier chapter, fundamental differences in the non-directive and the directive traditions. If these traditions involve different conceptions as to the roles of interviewer and interviewee which are not simply abstract conceptions, then significant differences should be revealed in the patterns of interaction of the various groups which were led by the non-directive and the directive psychologists.

The directive approach

None of the students involved in the training course had a background in directive methods of interviewing. Most of them had a largely non-directive psychoanalytic background. On the other hand, the psychologist who led groups C and D had a directive background. It was anticipated that this difference in backgrounds would reflect itself in the interaction of the leader and two groups. This was largely the case. The effects of this are fully discussed later in the chapter.

At the commencement of the role playing exercises, members of groups C and D were given a short lecture on the directive approach in an effort to minimize the degree of conflict between the psychologist's and their own background in the psychoanalytic, non-directive tradition. Students were asked to closely observe the extent to which interviewers adopted the directive as against the non-directive approach. They were, however, not instructed to adopt consciously one or the other approach, but to feel their way into the interviews while being conscious of the reactions of their colleagues within the interview situation.

Description of the directive groups

The two groups which were led by the directive psychologist were groups C and D. These two groups differed in their cohesiveness at the commencement of the role playing exercises. Group C was no more than a collection of nine separate and distinct individuals who had been brought together only for the role playing sessions. They lacked a group identity and reflected this in their comments. They reflected much hostility against each other but directed it mainly at one particular individual within the group. Group D, on the other hand, was a fairly cohesive group of people. This difference between groups C and D was observed even by the members themselves.

Task materials

The students in groups C and D participated in two role playing sessions. The first session was more structured than the second. The students were given different roles on pieces of paper which they had to activate in pairs—one person playing the role of interviewer and the other playing the role of interviewee. These roles were largely confined to those which probation officers would normally experience during the course of their work—prison welfare officer, probation officer, youthful delinquent, magistrate, etc. The obligations of each role were clearly explained to the students by the psychologist and the background contexts in which these roles would be activated in real life were also carefully discussed. These explanations were not only aimed at explaining the sorts of action which should be adopted during the role playing exercises but was also aimed at structuring the role playing sessions so closely that flexibility of action would be kept to the minimum. The interaction during this session was confined to pairs.

In the second session, the roles which were to be played were distributed orally and the background characteristics of each role were only very sketchily explained. The students were then instructed to apply their personal comprehension and knowledge of the obligations attached to these roles and to adopt those patterns of action which they felt were appropriate. Unlike the first session, in which full details of the role obligations and contexts for action were provided, students were provided only with the bare outlines of the obligations that pertained to the specified roles. The greater degree of structuring in the first session was aimed at forcing the students to conform to the obligations of the roles which were dictated to them whereas the second, unstructured, session was aimed at forcing the students to dissolve their own personal identities in the roles which they were playing during the exercises. It was felt that their personal emotions would be released by not restricting their actions to a set format during the second session. Emotions are easily concealed where actions are restricted to a set format. In order to emphasize the educational value of the exercise to the students, it was necessary to allow them to employ aspects of their own personal identities in the execution of the obligations of roles.

Further, whereas the first session utilized two-person groups, the second session utilized three-person groups, in an effort to create group interviewing situations in which one person would interview more than one respondent simultaneously. It was felt that the educational experience of interviewing which can be obtained from role playing can only be realized where students are exposed to personal interview situations as well as to group interviewing situations, even though the students were conscious of the artifically contrived nature of those situations. In general, the students were allowed to decide whether to play the roles of interviewer or interviewee. After a short period had elapsed, the roles of interviewer and interviewee were reversed in order to ensure that each student experienced the emotional implications of being both interviewer and interviewee respectively.

Procedure: session 1

The students were given specific roles to play. These roles were written out on pieces of paper and distributed to the two groups. Pairs of students were selected to act as interviewers and interviewees respectively, and each pair performed the role playing exercises independently of the others. Those students who were waiting their turn were hidden from the sight of the pair which was role playing by the short leg of an 'L'-shaped room but were able to observe the proceedings by means of closed-circuit television equipment.

Each pair of students acted out their specified roles for approximately fifteen to twenty minutes before the roles were reversed. The entire performance was recorded on video-tape for subsequent evaluation and discussion by the students as a whole and by the psychologist who was in charge.

When all the students in both groups had played their respective roles, a thirty-minute discussion was held on the role playing exercises in the first session. The students commented on their experiences during the course of the role playing exercises while the psychologist evaluated each performance in terms of the techniques which were applied.

Procedure: session 2

For the second session, the students in both groups were split up into groups of threes and were instructed orally about the roles which were to be performed. They were then asked to discuss the obligations attached to each role amongst themselves and to decide who should play which roles. The involvement of the psychologist was restricted to the preliminary briefing when the roles which should be played in the role exercises were distributed, but neither the obligations that are attached to these roles nor the contexts in which these roles are usually activated in normal life were discussed. Accordingly, the psychologist was not involved in the discussion amongst students of the obligations attached to each role.

Each three-person group of role performers did their role playing exercises away from the rest of the group who were waiting to take their turns. But those students who were not, at any time, taking part in the role exercises were deliberately kept out of the range of hearing of those who were. This was done in order to reduce the range of possible distractions for those who were involved, at any one time, in the exercise of role playing. The proceedings of this session, as in the case of those in session one, were video-taped but closed-circuit television equipment was not used to relay these proceedings live to the remaining students who were awaiting their turns.

The video-tape equipment was invaluable in providing an opportunity for all students to discuss the performances at the end of the exercises. The ideal situation would have been to use a two-way mirror so that those students who, at any one time, were not engaged in role playing could view the situation live and so be enabled to recognize the development of crises situations among those who were actively engaged in the exercise and note the extent to which personal idiosyncrasies were involved in the interpretation of the obligations attached to roles. This facility was, however, not available. The video-tape equipment which was used therefore provided a substitute of sorts for a two-way mirror.

Each student was allowed to enact the actions attached to any particular role for fifteen to twenty minutes, after which roles were transferred. As three-person groups were involved, each interviewer dealt with two of their colleagues as repondents at any one time. The roles of interviewer and respondent were then rotated so as to provide equal opportunities for all students to activate both the roles of interviewer and interviewee respectively.

At the end of this second session of role playing the students were brought together to view the video-tape of their performances and to discuss these with the psychologist who was in charge.

Simulated interview situations

A number of interview situations taken from case histories, were simulated in both sessions. The degree of descriptive detail as to the attendant obligations of both interviewer and client differed; in the first session, much of the descriptive detail was provided by the psychologist, whereas in the second session, only very brief detail of these obligations was provided. The students had to interpret the role obligations of the various roles for themselves. A representative sample of the interview situations which were simulated in the role playing exercises in this session were as follows:

1 A prison interview in which the assistance of a social worker is sought by an inmate who is anxious to know about the domestic situation he left behind him; he had not heard from his family for several weeks.
2 A prison interview by a probation officer of a prospective parolee who had been convicted for cashing dud cheques on an out-dated banking account. The inmate was both a qualified engineer and a vicar.
3 A matrimonial counselling situation in which a probation officer interviews a couple whose matrimonial problems revolve around sexual matters.
4 A matrimonial counselling situation in which the husband wishes to preserve and continue his marriage whereas the wife desires a separation and divorce.
5 A probation officer who attempts to enforce parole conditions; one such condition prohibited two criminal homosexuals from associating with each other because of their past joint criminal activities. The homosexuals, on the other hand, attribute this condition on their parole to the fact of their being homosexuals which, in fact, is not the case.
6 A family interview situation by a probation officer with the parents of a young offender.

7 A regular office interview of a probationer.

The two situations which elicited the greatest amount of emotional involvement and discussion in the groups which did them were the fourth one concerning the wife who wanted a divorce and the fifth one concerning the two criminal homosexuals.

Results and discussion

The second session of role playing exercises yielded better results for both groups than the first session. This can be attributed, first, to the greater freedom of expression which students were allowed in the second session and the extent to which this invoked their emotional involvement. All the students were engaging in role play for the first time during the first session of these exercises; they may, for this reason, have been more inhibited by the artificial character of the exercises as well as by the setting in which the training course took place. By the time they came round to the second session, they were more relaxed and freer in their emotional interactions with each other. This accounts, in part, for the more positive results from the second session compared to the first. Second, the role playing exercises in the second session were closer to real life situations because the amount of elaboration provided by the psychologists initially was kept to a minimum. The students were therefore forced to involve their own identities in those inherent in the roles which they were playing to a much greater extent than would otherwise be the case and thereby eliminated the gulf between play-acting and actual role behaviour. A third possibility is that the students may have simply learned how to act out roles by the time they came to the second session so that the better results from this session reflected the effect of practice; this is a possibility which cannot be ruled out.

Interviewers in the second session found it more difficult to control interviewee behaviour, as is often the case in real life group interviewing situations. This was largely because the three-person interaction that was involved in the second session invoked a greater degree of emotional involvement among participants than was the case with the two-person groups in the first session. As they progressed through the second session, they found it increasingly difficult to separate fact from fiction as far as their role playing was concerned.

Both role playing sessions had definitive effects on both groups C and D, for it turned them from being two relatively loose collections of individuals into two very cohesive groups. Group C, in particular, lacked any degree of cohesiveness at the commencement of the role playing sessions. After handling the homosexual situation, they developed a higher level of group identity. This was such that when the video-tape was subsequently replayed to the whole training course, one of its members felt impelled to leave the room in case the assembled audience laughed, not at the performances captured on video-tape but, as he put it, 'at the members of the family who produced it'.

One emphasis in the discussions during the role playing exercises, as well as afterwards, was on the difference between non-directive and directive counselling and on the extent to which apparently non-directive interviewers often employ directive considerations without being aware that they are doing so. Those who recognized this, nevertheless confessed their fear of exploiting these considerations but recognized its advantages over non-directive counselling, especially in interview situations dealing with the case of the husband who wishes to preserve his marriage against the inclinations of his wife, and the homosexuals who were to be prevented from associating with each other.

The non-directive approach

Groups A and B were led by a psychologist with a non-directive and Freudian background, and the approach adopted during the role playing exercises was non-directive. The students were instructed on various ways of eliciting and assessing information from clients and were warned against asking leading questions which call forth definitive responses from clients.

Description of the non-directive groups

The two groups involved were relatively cohesive groups before they entered the role playing situation. This was partly due to the fact that their members had experienced some interaction with each other before the role playing part of the training course commenced. There was no overt hostility among group members and they got on well with the psychologist who was in charge.

Task materials

The same task materials were used with these groups of students as were used with groups C and D under the directive psychologist. The students in these groups—A and B—had to choose between two types of interviewing; role play using situations written out on strips of paper, as in the case of the directive groups, and personal interviews in which students interviewed each other on aspects of their personal lives. Most students chose the latter type. All the interviews were carried out in two-person groups in the presence of students who were awaiting their turns. Two sessions were used in order to cope with the numbers of students involved in the two groups, but the conditions under which these sessions were carried out did not differ between the first and the second sessions.

Procedure

Each pair of students had to decide whether they would employ role playing situations or personal interview situations dealing with their personal lives. They then discussed the obligations of specified roles in the case of those who elected to employ role playing situations and decided on who was to act as interviewer and as interviewee respectively. The role playing situations and the personal interview situations were allowed to run for fifteen to twenty minutes before roles were reversed. The proceedings were recorded on video-tape equipment. At the end of each session, all the students who participated were brought together to view the video-taped material on the proceedings as in the case of the directive groups.

Interview situations

Most of the interview situations simulated were of the personal interview type as against the role playing type. A sample of the situations employed were:

1 An office interview with a client who had been arrested for shoplifting.
2 An interview by a probation officer with a parent of a delinquent youth, with a view to deciding on the type of custody and access which would be appropriate.
3 An interview with a probationer who requires a job.
4 One student played the part of the most difficult client he had ever worked with.

Most students found these interviews relatively easy to handle as they were closely related to situations in which they had been involved in the course of their work.

Results and discussion

All the students in both groups considered that the personal interview is best suited to the exploration of the emotional background of clients; they also felt that the client's perception of the interviewer is best explored by means of the personal interview. However, both groups were preoccupied with a fear of revealing professional incompetence as interviewers on the one hand and giving away too much information of a personal nature as interviewees on the other.

The discussion concentrated on the 'type' of person that is exhibited by an interviewer and how this could affect the client's responses. One student reflected a hearty and warm personality with whom a client could readily and easily identify himself. A female probation officer used her Christian religious beliefs as an aid to her assessment of the needs of clients and reflected a moral and Christian personality type as a consequence; another revealed little of her own self and allowed the client to structure the relationship that emerged during the course of her interview. Another student reflected a very conceited and arrogant personality type and was generally criticized by his colleagues for this stance. By the end of the discussion period, the cohesiveness which characterized both groups initially had disappeared and their group identities were lost.

Conclusion

On the second day of the role play sessions, the entire course membership was brought together for an evaluation of this section of the training course. The video-tape interview of the probation officer and the two homosexuals was shown to the assembled audience because of the high degree of emotional involvement of all participants and the skill of those who acted as interviewers. Members of groups C and D—the directive groups—sat together and supported each other throughout the course of the evaluation. Groups A and B, however, did not locate themselves in any definite pattern among the members of the audience and were hostile to the non-directive psychologist who had been in charge of their groups.

This difference in the responses of the directive and the non-directive groups can be explained partly in terms of the extent to which groups maintained their identity throughout the role playing sessions and during the general discussion, and partly by the fact that the directive psychologist set himself up as a hate object for each of his two groups within the first few minutes of meeting them, thereby providing them with someone outside of both groups against whom they could turn their emotions. The alternative would have been to contain such emotions within the groups to the detriment of group solidarity. This can be an important factor when dealing with groups in therapeutic situations, for the object of counselling is not to destroy the group but to change it by personal influence. Although the directive psychologist produced a situation at the beginning of the sessions in which all hostility within groups can be directed outwards towards him, he was nevertheless evaluated in a friendly way during the discussion as well as afterwards.

Groups A and B, on the other hand, were hostile towards the non-directive psychologist who had been in charge of them and did not support each other during the discussion period with the whole course membership. Largely because of their hostility towards the psychologist and towards each other, they tended to view their own participation in the role playing sessions as having been less than useful.

One year after the course, a follow-up check on the students who had participated in the role playing sessions (all four groups taken together) showed that participation in these sessions had proved to be of benefit to probation officers in course of their work. Eighty-five per cent replied that these sessions had helped them and fifteen per cent stated that they had not derived any noticeable benefit from their having participated in these sessions. In general, those students who had the non-directive psychologist felt that a more directive approach on his part might have been more useful for their purposes.

In sum, role playing provides an opportunity for students to see themselves in interviewing situations and be able to learn from errors without involving real clients who may be disturbed by relating to inexperienced interviewers. It can be used in any context. But its usefulness must depend on the availability of specific aids such as two-way mirrors, closed-circuit television and video-tape equipment.

10

Summary and conclusions

It would be a mistake to regard this book as providing an exhaustive treatment of both interviewing and communication. An exhaustive treatment of two extensive areas such as these would call for a much wider exploration of the themes that have been touched upon, since both subjects have received considerable attention from a range of otherwise unrelated disciplines. Interviewing on the one hand, is an activity which is relevant to a number of professional fields and disciplines other than social work and, to a lesser extent in this work, psychotherapy. On the other hand, the subject of communication by itself has been examined by a number of disciplines because it plays an important part not only in the organization of society but also in many of the technological developments which have been undertaken in this century. There is no room in a small book such as this one for an exhaustive analysis of the way in which these subjects have been considered in all professional contexts as well as for tracing every aspect of their interrelationship in the specific context of social work. Such a project would require a completely different approach from the one which has been adopted here.

The main objective of this work is much less ambitious and much more realistic. It is not concerned with presenting a comprehensive coverage of all the issues which are relevant to a consideration of interviewing and communication but is restricted to highlighting the significant extent which both interviewing and communication are, and must remain, central to the activities of the social worker in particular and to the whole series of professions which are often characterized as the 'caring' professions in general. There is, indeed a serious sense in which it can be said with Irvine (1955, p. 13) that the word 'communication' sums up the whole of the casework process, for not only does it involve the development of adequate relationships between the caseworker and the client but it also

163

requires a systematic process of structuring thought, language and emotional feeling. The whole process must understandably, therefore, invoke the operation of a range of subtle psychological processes in both the social worker and the client. These processes must, equally understandably, operate within the context of the social norms and values which define and characterize interaction in any society. This, in effect, ensures that the interaction between a worker and a client in a casework relationship must reflect the general characteristics as well as linguistic codes which are found in that particular society.

This means, to a certain extent, that the casework relationship must be regarded as being somewhat bound by the wider characteristics of the society within which it occurs. It also means that caseworkers with different cultural and social backgrounds operating with clients from other cultural and social backgrounds must experience or, at least, be aware of the extent to which frustrations in communication can arise.

Such frustrations need not necessarily turn on the matter of language as this is usually understood; it is not a straightforwardly simple matter as to whether the client comprehends the English language or not or, indeed, whether the caseworker comprehends German (if the client speaks only German); languages are verbal forms of communication which are relatively specific to linguistic communities. Other more important elements in the frustrations which can occur concern the modes of thinking, gestural articulation as well as the verbalization of feeling and emotion which underpin the use of language. These are the elements of which language comprehension is no more than the 'tip of the iceberg'. The 'tip' is certainly important but should not detract from the much larger body of the problem of communication which consists of linguistic nuances, tones, gestures, bodily and mental responses and perception. It is among these elements that the source of all frustration resides.

The preceding chapters have been aimed at exploring these elements. They require to be structured in some way during the activity of interviewing. They never, in themselves, appear in a structured and systematic way. If this was otherwise, the task of the social worker would not be the problematic one that it is, but could be made much simpler by classifying different people into a number of predetermined categories before an interview and by deducing from such categories how specific individuals would react in the interview situation. Nature is, however, rather unkind in this respect, for the problematic interrelationship of these elements imposes the burden of structuring on the caseworker. It is when the caseworker proceeds to attempt this structuring process that the complexity of communication and interviewing is brought into sharp relief. This complexity is made even more starkly evident where few assumptions can be made about the social and cultural pressures of the background of both the social worker and the client. Does this mean, in effect, that the close link between the interviewing process and the background social factors within which it must operate demands that all interviews must be specific to specific societies or countries or peoples? Does this mean, in other words, that only Asian interviewers can adequately interact with Asian clients, British interviewers with British clients, working-class interviewers with working-class clients?

The answer must, most evidently, be in the negative for the inherent relativity in the interviewing process lends itself to a limited degree of generalization. The different nationalities, ethnic groups, social classes, etc., are not so thoroughly different from each other that their responses to the interviewing situation must be completely unique to each one. This is so not only because of the common human element which is involved in communication but also because all interviews possess denominators which are common and which provide a common foundation for the interaction of interviewers and clients of different nationalities, ethnic groups and social classes. The preceding chapters would have emphasized that while interviewing across social and cultural categories invokes the common denominators which were delineated, nevertheless there are various 'pressures' which can be introduced into the interviewing process of which one must be aware. Our discussion was aimed at demonstrating the importance of some of these elements and the effect which they could have in the interview situation. It was also aimed at demonstrating that these pressures are so general that they create problematic issues within the interview situation for *both* interviewer and client.

The earlier and more theoretical chapters showed that the general nature of the interview and its application to a wide range of professions does not deny its possession of certain common elements which are found in all interviews. It further stressed that these common denominators must therefore provide the point of departure for obtaining an understanding of the complexities which can arise in the interviewing process. It also examined specific cultural and subcultural factors—race and ethnicity, linguistic codes and thought processes, gestural forms and bodily movements—as well as specific psychological processes which could be problematic in the interview situation. The later and more practical chapters dealt with a range of considerations which must influence the interviewer's orientation towards the task of interviewing and which are important in the appropriate setting. It is in this connection that the different traditions of interviewing which originally derived from psychotherapy were discussed, for the application of these traditions do not change the nature of the interview; they do not destroy the common denominators to which we alluded; they are, on the contrary, imposed on these common denominators and define the activities and orientations of both client and interviewer.

Bibliography

Asterisks denote articles and books recommended for further reading.

*ACKERMAN, N. (1966) *Treating the Troubled Family*, Basic Books, New York.

ADORNO, T. W. *et al.* (1950) *The Authoritarian Personality*, Harper, New York.

ALLPORT, F. H. (1962) 'A structuronomic conception of behaviour: individual and collective. I. Structural theory and the master problem of social psychology', *Journal of Abnormal and Social Psychology*, Vol. 64, pp. 258-90.

*ALPINE, G. C. *et al.* (1965) 'Interviewing techniques for social work student training', *Mental Hygiene*, Vol. 49, No. 1, pp. 126-31.

ARDREY, R. (1967) *The Territorial Imperative: A Personal Inquiry into the Animal Origins of Property and Nations*, Collins, London.

*ARGYLE, M. (1967) *The Psychology of Interpersonal Behaviour*, Penguin Books, London.

—— (1969) *Social Interaction*, Methuen, London.

*BATESON, G. (1972) *Steps to an Ecology of Mind*, Ballantine, New York.

*BENNEY, M. *et al.* (1956) 'Age and sex in the interview', *American Journal of Sociology*, Vol. 62, pp. 143-52.

BERG, C. (1955) *The First Interview with a Psychiatrist*, Allen & Unwin, London.

BERNE, E. (1964) *Games People Play*, Grove Press, New York.

BERNSTEIN, B. (1958) 'Some sociological determinants of perception', *British Journal of Sociology*, Vol. 9, pp. 159-74.

—— (1959) 'A public language: Some sociological implications of a linguistic form', *British Journal of Sociology*, Vol. 10, pp. 311-26.

—— (1960) 'Language and social class', *British Journal of Sociology*, Vol. 11, pp. 271-6.

—— (1961) 'Social structure, language and learning', *Educational Research*, Vol. 3, pp. 163-76.

—— (1962a) 'Linguistic codes, hesitation phenomena and intelligence', *Language and Speech*, Vol. 5, pp. 31-46.

167

BERNSTEIN, B. (1962b) 'Social class, linguistic codes and grammatical elements', *Language and Speech*, Vol. 5, pp. 221-40.

—— (1964) 'Aspects of Language and Learning in the Genesis of the Social Process' in D. Hymes, ed., *Language in Culture and Society*, Harper & Row, New York, pp. 251-63.

—— (1965a) 'Social Class and Linguistic Development: A Theory of Social Learning', in A. H. Halsey, J. Floud and C. A. Anderson, eds, *Education, Economy and Society*, Free Press, New York, pp. 288-314.

—— (1965b) 'A Socio-Linguistic Approach to Social Learning', in J. Gould, ed., *Penguin Survey of the Social Sciences*, Penguin Books, London.

—— (1969) 'Social Class Differences in Communication and Control', in W. Brandis and D. Henderson, eds, *Social Class, Language and Communication*, Routledge & Kegan Paul, London.

*—— (1971) *Class, Codes and Control: Theoretical Studies Towards a Sociology of Language*, Vol. 1, Routledge & Kegan Paul, London.

*—— (1972) 'Social Class, Language and Socialization', in N. Minnis, ed., *Linguistics at Large*, Gollancz, London, pp. 230-45.

BERNSTEIN, B. and BRANDIS, W. (1969) 'Social class differences in the relevance of language to socialization', *Sociology*, Vol. 3, pp. 1-20.

BERNSTEIN, B. and YOUNG, D. (1966) 'Some Aspects of the Relationship Between Communication and Performance in Tests', in J. E. Meade and S. Parkes, eds, *Genetic and Environmental Factors in Human Ability*, Oliver & Boyd, London.

*BESSELL, R. (1972) *Interviewing and Counselling*, Batsford, London.

*BETTINGHAUS, E. (1968) *Persuasive Communication*, Holt, Rinehart & Winston, New York.

*BINGHAM, W. V. *et al.* (1959) *How to Interview*, Harper & Row, New York.

BIRDWHISTELL, R. L. (1963) 'The Kinesic Level in the Investigation of the Emotions', in P. Knapp, ed., *Expression of the Emotions in Man*, International Universities Press, New York.

BOGARDUS, E. (1936) *Introduction to Social Research*, Sutton House, Los Angeles.

BONHAM, J. D. (1954) *The Middle Class Vote*, Faber & Faber, London.

BOTT, E. (1971) *Family and Social Network* (second edition), Tavistock Publications, London.

BOWLBY, J. (1965) *Child Care and the Growth of Love*, Penguin Books, London.

—— (1971) *Attachment and Loss*, Vol. 1, Penguin Books, London.

BOX, S. and FORDE, J. (1971) 'The facts don't fit: on the relationship between social class and criminal behaviour', *Sociological Review*, Vol. 19, No. 1, pp. 31-52.

BRAYFIELD, A. ed. (1950) *Readings in Modern Methods of Counselling*, Appleton-Century-Crofts, New York.

BROWN, R. (1959) *Words and Things*, Free Press, New York.

—— (1965) *Social Psychology*, Collier-Macmillan, London.

BRUNER, J. S. and TAGUIRI, R. (1954) 'The Perception of People', in G.

Lindzey, ed., *Handbook of Social Psychology*, Vol. 2, Addison-Wesley, New York.

*CARKHUFF, R. R. (1969) *Helping and Human Relations*, Vols 1 and 2, Holt, Rinehart & Winston, New York.

CARKHUFF, R. R. and BERENSON, B. (1967) *Sources of Gain in Counselling and Psychotherapy*, Holt, Rinehart & Winston, Toronto.

CARROLL, J. ed. (1956) *Language Thought and Reality: Selected Writings of Benjamin Lee Whorf*, MIT/Wiley, New York.

CHAPPLE, E. D. (1953) 'The standard interview as used in interaction chronograph investigations', *Human Organization*, Vol. 12, No. 2, pp. 22-32.

CHEETHAM, J. (1972) *Social Work With Immigrants*, Routledge & Kegan Paul, London.

CHERRY, C. (1957) *On Human Communication: a Review, a Survey and a Criticism*, MIT Press, Massachusetts.

*CICOUREL, A. (1964) *Method and Measurement in Sociology*, Ch. 3, Free Press, New York.

COLCORD, J. (1929) 'A study of techniques of the social case work interview', *Journal of Social Forces*, Vol. VII, pp. 519-27.

COOK, M. (1971) *Interpersonal Perception*, Penguin Books, London.

COTGROVE, S. (1967) *The Science of Society*, Allen & Unwin, London.

CROSS, C. P. (1969) 'The Sense of Identity of West African Students', Ph.D. thesis, unpublished, London School of Economics, University of London.

*DANIEL, W. W. (1968) *Racial Discrimination in England*, Penguin Books, London.

DAVIS, K. (1940) 'Extreme social isolation of a child', *American Journal of Sociology*, Vol. 45, pp. 554-65.

*—— (1948) *Human Society*, Macmillan, New York.

DAWTRY, F. ed. (1968) *The Social Problems of Drug Abuse*, Butterworth, London.

*DAY, P. (1972) *Communication in Social Work*, Pergamon Press, London, Ch. 3.

DEUTSCH, M. (1965) 'The role of social class in language development and cognition', *American Journal of Orthopsychiatry*, Vol. 35, No. 1, pp. 78-88.

DJILAS, M. (1957) *The New Class*, Praeger, New York.

DOHRENWEND, B. and CHIN-SHONG, E. (1967) 'Social status and attitudes towards psychological disorder: the problem of tolerance of deviance', *American Sociological Review*, Vol. 32, pp. 417-33.

*DOUGLAS, J. W. B. (1964) *The Home and the School*, MacGibbon & Kee, London.

DUNCAN, H. D. (1967) 'The Search for a Social Theory of Communication in American Sociology', in Frank E. Dance, ed., *Human Communication Theory: Original Essays*, Holt, Rinehart & Winston, New York, p. 252.

ECKMAN, P. *et al.* (1969) 'Pan-cultural elements in facial displays of emotion', *Science*, Vol. 164, No. 3875.

169

EHRENKRANZ, S. (1967) 'A study of joint interviewing in the treatment of marital problems', Parts 1 and 2, *Social Casework*, Vol. LXVIII, Nos 8 and 9.

*EHRLICH, J. S. and RIESMAN, D. (1961) 'Age and authority in the interview', *Public Opinion Quarterly*, Vol. 25, pp. 39-56.

ELDRED, S. H. and PRICE, D. (1958) 'Linguistic evaluation of feeling states in psychotherapy', *Psychiatry*, Vol. 21, pp. 115-21.

ELLIS, A. (1957) 'Outcome of employing three techniques of psychotherapy', *Journal of Clinical Psychology*, Vol. 23, pp. 344-50.

ENGLISH, H. and B. (1958) *A Comprehensive Dictionary of Psychological and Psychoanalytical Terms*, Longmans Green, London.

ETKIN, W. (1963) 'Communication among Animals', in Jon Eisenson, ed., *The Psychology of Communication*, Appleton-Century-Crofts.

EYSENCK, H. J. (1954) *The Psychology of Politics*, Routledge & Kegan Paul, London.

*—— (1961) 'The Effects of Psychotherapy', in Eysenck, ed., *Handbook of Abnormal Psychology*, Basic Books, New York, pp. 697-725.

—— (1965) *Fact and Fiction in Psychology*, Penguin Books, London.

*FAST, J. (1971) *Body Language*, Simon Schuster, Toronto, and Penguin Books, London.

*FEAR, R. (1958) *The Evaluation Interview*, McGraw-Hill, New York.

FEARING, F. (1954) 'An Examination of the Conceptions of Benjamin Lee Whorf in the Light of Theories of Perception and Cognition', in H. Hoijer, ed., *Language in Culture*, Chicago University Press.

—— (1964) 'Human Communication', in Lewis Dexter and D. M. White, eds, *People, Society and Mass Communications*, Free Press, New York.

*FENLASON, A. et al. (1962) *Essentials in Interviewing*, Harper & Row, New York.

FERARD, M. and HUNNYBUN, N. (1962) *The Caseworker's Use of Relationships*, Tavistock Publications, London.

FESTINGER, L. (1950) 'Informal social communication', *Psychological Review*, Vol. 57, pp. 271-82.

FIELD, F. and HAIKIN, P., eds (1971) *Black Britons*, Oxford University Press, London.

*FLOUD, F. and HALSEY, A. (1956) *Social Class and Educational Opportunity*, Heinemann, London.

*FORD, D. H. and URBAN, H. (1963) *Systems of Psychotherapy: A Comparative Study*, Wiley, New York.

FORDE, J. (1968) *Social Class and the Comprehensive School*, Routledge & Kegan Paul, London.

*FREUD, S. (1960) *Jokes and their Relationship to the Unconscious*, Routledge & Kegan Paul, London.

GARFIELD, S. (1971) 'Research on Client Variables in Psychotherapy', in A. Bergin and S. Garfield, eds, *Handbook of Psychotherapy and Behaviour Change: An Empirical Analysis*, Wiley, New York.

GLASSER, W. (1965) *Reality Therapy: A New Approach to Psychiatry*, Harper & Row, New York.

GLEASON, H. A. (1961) *An Introduction to Descriptive Linguistics*, Holt, Rinehart & Winston, New York.

—— (1965) *Linguistics and English Grammar*, Holt, Rinehart & Winston, New York.

GOFFMANN, E. (1956-7) 'Embarrassment and social organisation', *American Journal of Sociology*, Vol. 62, pp. 264-71.

—— (1963) *Behaviour in Public Places*, Free Press, New York.

—— (1972) *Encounters*, Penguin Books, London.

GOULD, J. (1971) 'A Sociological Portrait of Nationality and Ethnicity', *New Society*, No. 483, pp. 1281-4.

GREENBERG, J. (1966) *Language Universals*, Mouton, The Hague.

HAGGARD, F. A. and ISAACS, K. (1966) 'Micro-momentary Facial Expressions as Indicators of Ego-Mechanisms in Psychotherapy', in L. A. Gottschalk and A. H. Auerbach, eds, *Methods of Research in Psychotherapy*, Appleton-Century-Crofts, New York.

*HALL, E. T. (1969) *The Hidden Dimension*, Doubleday Anchor Books, New York.

—— (1971) *The Silent Language*, Random House, New York.

*HARPER, R. A. (1959) *Psychoanalysis and Psychotherapy: 36 Systems*, Prentice Hall, New Jersey.

HARLOW, H. F. (1958) 'The nature of love', *American Psychologist*, Vol. 13, pp. 73-85.

HARLOW, H. and M. (1962) 'Social deprivation in monkeys', *Scientific American*, Vol. 207, No. 5, pp. 136-46.

HARTLEY, R. and E. (1964) 'The Importance and Nature of Communication' in C. Steinberg, ed., *Mass Media and Communication*, Free Press, New York.

HEIDER, F. and G. (1940) 'A comparison of sentence structure of deaf and hearing children', *Psychological Monograph*, Vol. 52, No. 1, pp. 42-103.

HERAUD, B. (1970) *Sociology and Social Work: Perspectives and Problems*, Pergamon, London.

HEYWOOD, J. (1964) *An Introduction to Teaching Casework Skills*, Routledge & Kegan Paul, London.

HILBOURNE, J. (1972) 'Social class and the residential social rehabilitation of newly-blind adult males', *British Journal of Social Work*, Vol. 2, No. 2, pp. 127-41.

HIRO, D. (1971) *Black British, White British*, Eyre & Spottiswoode, London.

HOGGART, R. (1957) *The Uses of Literacy*, Chatto & Windus, London.

HOLLINGSHEAD, A. and REDLICH, F. (1958) *Social Class and Mental Illness*, Wiley, New York.

HYMAN, H. (1954a) *Interviewing in Social Research*, University of Chicago Press.

—— (1954b) 'The Value Systems of Different Classes: A Social Psychological Contribution to the Analysis of Social Stratification', in R. Bendix and S. Lipset, eds, *Class, Status and Power*, Routledge & Kegan Paul, London, pp. 426-42.

IRVINE, M. (1955) 'Communication and relationship in social casework', *Social Casework*, Vol. XXXVI, No. 1, pp. 13-21.

*JACKSON, B. and MARSDEN, D. (1962) *Education and the Working Class*, Routledge & Kegan Paul, London.

JAGANNHADHAM, V. (1965) 'Social Policy and Social Work', in S. K. Khinduka, ed., *Social Work in India*, Kitab Mahal, Allahabad, pp. 135-61.

JORDAN, W. (1972) *The Social Worker in Family Situations*, Routledge & Kegan Paul, London.

JOURARD, S. (1966) 'An exploratory study of body-accessibility', *British Journal of Social and Clinical Psychology*, Vol. 46, pp. 130-8.

KAHN, R. and CANNELL, C. (1957) *The Dynamics of Interviewing: Theory, Technique and Cases*, Wiley, New York.

KENDALL, D. C. (1957) 'Mental Development of Young Deaf Children', in A. E. Ewing, ed., *Educational Guidance and the Deaf Child*, Manchester University Press.

*KEPHART, N. G. (1952) *The Employment Interview in Industry*, McGraw-Hill, New York.

*KERR, M. (1958) *The People of Ship Street*, Routledge & Kegan Paul, London.

KINSEY, A. C. *et al.* (1948) *Sexual Behaviour in the Human Male*, Saunders, Philadelphia.

*KLEIN, J. (1965) *Samples from English Cultures*, Routledge & Kegan Paul, London, Vol. 2, pp. 537ff.

KLEIN, P. (1968) *From Philanthropy to Social Welfare: An American Cultural Perspective*, Jossey-Bass, San Francisco.

KLUCKHOHN, C. and MURRAY, H., eds (1948) *Personality in Nature, Society and Culture*, Knopf, New York.

*KOGAN, L. S. (1950) 'The electrical recording of social casework interviews', *Social Casework*, Vol. 31, pp. 371-8.

*KRASNER, P. (1961) *Impolite Interviews*, Lyle Stuart, New York.

KURTZ, K. and HOVLAND, C. (1953) 'The effect of verbalization during observation of stimulus objects upon accuracy of recognition and recall', *Journal of Experimental Psychology*, Vol. 45, pp. 157-64.

*LAING, R. D. (1960) *The Divided Self*, Tavistock Publications, London.

—— (1961) *Self and Others*, Tavistock Publications, London.

*—— (1971) *Knots*, Penguin Books, London.

LAMBERT, R. and BRESSLER, M. (1954) 'The sensitive area complex: a contribution to a theory of guided culture contact', *American Journal of Sociology*, Vol. 60, pp. 583-92.

LANG, O. (1946) *Chinese Family and Society*, Yale University Press, New Haven.

LAWTON, D. (1963) 'Social class differences in language development: a study of some samples of written work', *Language and Speech*, Vol. 6, pp. 120-43.

—— (1970) *Social Class, Language and Education*, Routledge & Kegan Paul, London.

*LEE, D. J. (1968) 'Class differentials in educational opportunity and promotions from the ranks', *Sociology*, Vol. 2, No. 3, pp. 293-312.

*LEONARD, P. (1965) 'Social control, class values and social work practice', Social Work, Vol. 22, No. 4, pp. 9-13.

LEWIN, K. (1951) Field Theory in Social Science, ed. D. Cartwright, Harper & Row, New York.

LIPSET, S. (1963) Political Man, Doubleday Anchor Books, New York.

LONDON, P. (1964) The Modes and Morals of Psychotherapy, Holt, Rinehart & Winston, New York.

*LUBOVE, R. (1965) The Professional Altruist: The Emergence of Social Work as a Career 1880-1930, Harvard University Press, Massachusetts.

LURIA, A. R. (1957) 'The Role of Language in the Formation of Temporary Connections', in Brian Simon, ed., Psychology in the Soviet Union, Routledge & Kegan Paul, London.

*MACCOBY, E. and N. (1954) 'The Interview: A Tool of Social Science', in G. Lindzey, ed., Handbook of Social Psychology, Vol. 1, Addison-Wesley, New York, pp. 449-87.

*MCCULLOCH, M. E. and ELY, P. (1968) Social Work with Groups, Routledge & Kegan Paul, London.

*MAHL, G. F. (1959) 'Measuring the patient's anxiety during interviews from "expressive" aspects of his speech', Transactions of the New York Academy of Science, Series 2, Vol. 21, pp. 249-59.

*MATARAZZO, J. D. et al. (1958) 'Psychological test and organismic correlates of interview interaction behaviour', Journal of Abnormal and Social Psychology, Vol. 56, pp. 329-38.

*—— (1962) 'Frequency and duration characteristics of speech and silence behaviour during interviews', Journal of Clinical Psychology, Vol. 18, pp. 416-26, McGraw-Hill, New York.

—— (1965) 'The Interview', in B. Wolman, ed., Handbook of Clinical Psychology, McGraw-Hill, New York, pp. 403-50.

*MAY, R. (1953) 'Historical and Philosophical Presuppositions for Understanding Therapy', in O. H. Mowrer, ed., Psychotherapy: Theory and Research, Ronald Press, New York, pp. 9-43.

MAYER, J. and TIMMS, N. (1970) The Client Speaks: Working Class Impressions of Casework, Routledge & Kegan Paul, London.

*MEAD, G. H. (1934) Mind, Self and Society, University of Chicago Press.

MEHRABIAN, A. (1960) 'The significance of posture and position in the communication of attitude and status relationships', Psychological Bulletin, Vol. 71, pp. 359-72.

*MERTON, R. and KENDALL, P. (1946) 'The focused interview', American Journal of Sociology, Vol. LI, pp. 541-57.

MILGRAM, S. (1963) 'Behavioural study of obedience', Journal of Abnormal and Social Psychology, Vol. 67, pp. 371-8.

*MITCHELL, C. (1959) 'Family interviewing in family diagnosis', Social Casework, Vol. XL, No. 7, pp. 381-4.

MOBBS, N. A. (1967) 'Eye Contact and Introversion-Extraversion', BA dissertation, unpublished, University of Reading.

MORRIS, D. (1967) The Naked Ape: A Zoologist's Study of the Human Animal, Jonathan Cape, London.

MORRISEY, J. (1953) 'A note on interviews with children facing imminent death', *Social Casework*, Vol. LXVI, No. 6, pp. 343-5.

*MORRISH, I. (1971) *The Sociology of Education: An Introduction*, Allen & Unwin, London. Especially chapter on education and stratification.

*MUSGRAVE, P. W. (1965) *The Sociology of Education*, Methuen, London, Ch. 5.

*MYERS, J. and BEAN, L. (1968) *A Decade Later: A Follow-Up of Social Class and Mental Illness*, Wiley, New York.

*NURSTEN, J. (1965) 'Social work, social class and speech systems', *Social Work*, Vol. 22, No. 4, pp. 3-8.

OGBURN, W. (1959) 'The wolf boy of Agra', *American Journal of Sociology*, Vol. 64, pp. 449-54.

OSGOOD, C. E. and SEBEOK, T., eds (1965) *Psycholinguistics: A Survey of Theory and Research Problems*, Indiana University Press, Bloomington.

OSTWALD, P. (1965) 'Acoustic methods in psychiatry', *Scientific American*, Vol. 212, pp. 82-91.

PARKIN, F. (1971) *Class Inequality and Political Order*, MacGibbon & Kee, London.

PARSONS, T. and SHILS, E., eds (1951) *Towards a General Theory of Action*, Harvard University Press, Mass.

PIAGET, J. (1945) *The Language and Thought of the Child*, Routledge & Kegan Paul, London.

*PITTINGER, R. E. *et al.* (1960) *The First Five Minutes: A Sample of Miscroscopic Interview Analysis*, Paul Martineau, Ithaca.

REYNOLDS, B. (1932) 'An experiment in short-contact interviewing', *Smith College Studies in Social Work*, Vol. III, September.

RICH, J. (1968) *Interviewing Children and Adolescents*, Macmillan, London.

*RIESMAN, D. (1958) 'Interviewers, elites and academic freedom', *Social Problems*, Vol. 6, pp. 115-26.

RILEY, M. and FLOWERMAN, S. (1951) 'Group relations as a variable in communications research', *American Sociological Review*, Vol. 16, pp. 174-80.

*ROBB, J. (1954) *Working Class Anti-Semite*, Tavistock Publications, London.

ROBINSON, D. and ROHDE, S. (1946) 'Two experiments with an anti-semitism poll', *Journal of Abnormal and Social Psychology*, Vol. 41, No. 2, pp. 136-44.

*ROGERS, C. (1945) 'The non-directive method as a technique for social research', *American Journal of Sociology*, Vol. L, pp. 279-88.

ROKEACH, M. (1960) *The Open and Closed Mind*, Basic Books, New York.

RUSSELL, C. and W. (1968) *Violence, Monkeys and Man*, Macmillan, London.

—— (1971) 'Language and Animal Signs', in N. Minnis, ed., *Linguistics at Large*, Gollancz, London, pp. 159-94.

*SALINGER, J. D. (1951) *The Catcher in the Rye*, Hamish Hamilton, London.

SALOMON, E. (1967) 'Humanistic Values and Social Casework', *Social Casework*, Vol. LXVIII, No. 1, Jan., pp. 26-32.

*SAPORTA, S., ed. (1961) *Psycholinguistics: A Book of Readings*, Holt, Rinehart & Winston, New York, Ch. 8.

SAUSSURE, F. DE (1916) *Cours de Linguistique Generale*, trans. W. Baskin, Owen, London.

SCHEFLEN, A. E. (1969) 'Non-language behaviour in communication'. Address to the New York Chapter of the American Academy of Pediatrics, New York, 2 Sept. (unpublished).

SCHLOSBERG, H. (1954) 'Three dimensions of emotion', *Psychological Review*, Vol. 61, pp. 81-8.

SCHUTZ, W. C. (1969) *Joy*, Grove Press, New York.

SECORD, P. (1959) 'Stereotyping and favorableness in the perception of negro faces', *Journal of Abnormal and Social Psychology*, Vol. 59, pp. 309-15.

SHEPARD, W. O. and SCHAEFFER, M. (1956) 'The effect of concept knowledge on Discrimination Learning', *Child Development*, Vol. 27, pp. 173-7.

*SHOSTAK, A. and GOMBERG, W., eds (1965) *Blue-Collar Worlds: Studies of the American Worker*, Prentice Hall, New Jersey.

SINGH, J. A. and ZINGG, R. (1943) *Wolf Children and Feral Man*, Harper, New York.

SKINNER, B. F. (1965) *Science and Human Behaviour*, Collier-Macmillan, New York.

SMIGEL, E. O. (1958) 'Interviewing a legal elite', *American Journal of Sociology*, Vol. LXIV, No. 2, pp. 159-64.

SMITH, A. ed. (1966) *Communication and Culture: Readings in the Codes of Human Interaction*, Holt, Rinehart & Winston, New York.

SOMMER, R. (1969) *Personal Space*, Prentice Hall, New Jersey.

*SPINLEY, B. (1953) *The Deprived and the Privileged: Personality Development in English Society*, Routledge & Kegan Paul, London.

*STORR, A. (1964) *Sexual Deviation*, Penguin Books, London.

STOUFFER, S. *et al.* (1949) *The American Soldier*, Princeton University Press, New Jersey, Vol. 4, p. 720.

*SULLIVAN, H. S. (1954) *The Psychiatric Interview*, Norton, New York.

TAYLOR, L. (1972) 'The significance and interpretation of replies to motivational questions: The case of sex offenders', *Sociology*, Vol. 6, pp. 23-39.

*TEMPLIN, M. C. (1957) *Certain Language Skills in Children: Their Development and Interrelationships*, University of Minnesota Press, Minneapolis, Ch. 8.

TIMMS, N. (1970) *Social Work: An Outline for the Intending Student*, Routledge & Kegan Paul, London.

*TRENCH, S. (1968) *Bury Me in My Boots*, Hodder & Stoughton, London.

TRISELIOTIS, J. ed. (1972) *Social Work With Coloured Immigrants and Their Families*, Oxford University Press for IRR, London.

VYGOTSKY, L. S. (1962) *Thought and Language*, MIT Press, Cambridge, Massachusetts.

BIBLIOGRAPHY

WEBER, M. (1970) *Max Weber: The Interpretation of Social Reality*, ed. J. E. Eldridge, Michael Joseph, London.

WILENSKY, H. and LEBEAUX, C. (1958) *Industrial Society and Social Welfare*, Russell Sage, New York.

*WOODROOFE, K. (1962) *From Charity to Social Work*, Routledge & Kegan Paul, London.

WOOTTON, B. (1959) *Social Science and Social Pathology*, Allen & Unwin, London.

YOUNG, A. F. and ASHTON, E. T. (1956) *British Social Work in the Nineteenth Century*, Routledge & Kegan Paul, London.

*YOUNG, P. V. (1935) *Interviewing in Social Work: A Sociological Analysis*, McGraw-Hill, New York.

YOUNGHUSBAND, E. ed. (1967) *Social Work and Social Values: Readings in Social Work*, Vol. III, Allen & Unwin, London.